Playing in the Dark

Rosie Dunn is formerly a crime reporter for the *Sun* and a journalist for the *News of the World*. She has worked as a freelance writer for the *Mail on Sunday*, *Daily Mail*, *Daily Mirror* and *Sunday Mirror* as well as national newspapers in Ireland.

Playing in the Dark

Siobhan Kennedy-McGuinness
with Rosie Dunn

arrow books

First published by Century 2010

This edition published by Arrow Books in 2011

2 4 6 8 10 9 7 5 3 1

First published in Great Britain in 2010 by
Century
The Random House Group Limited
20 Vauxhall Bridge Road, London, SW1V 2SA

www.rbooks.co.uk

The Random House Group Limited Reg. No. 954009

A CIP catalogue record for this book
is available from the British Library

ISBN 9780099519942

Addresses for companies within
The Penguin Random House Group can be found at:
global.penguinrandomhouse.com

Penguin Random House is committed to a sustainable future for
our business, our readers and our planet. This book is made from
Forest Stewardship Council® certified paper.

MIX
Paper from
responsible sources
FSC® C018179

Printed and bound in Great Britain by Clays Ltd, Elcograf S.p.A.

Typeset by SX Composing DTP, Rayleigh, Essex
Printed and bound in Great Britain by

This book is dedicated to my husband Derek and our four wonderful children. Thank you for everything.

It is also in loving memory of my beloved Gran, Mary Plunkett, and Thomas Dunn. May they both rest in peace.

Siobhan, age 7, Communion Day

Prologue

The man who stood before me, clutching the hands of two little children, looked scarcely any different. He was smaller and frailer than I had imagined him in my nightmares, but his cold, sinister eyes bored into me as though they were searing holes through my clothes and into my flesh.

He was as filthy, dishevelled and smelly as he had always been; his soiled and threadbare suit stained with cigarette ash – like a human nicotine stick that I wanted to crush and extinguish underneath my foot. I could see the grey-speckled tidemarks of dirt ingrained into his shirt collar, just as I had twenty years ago. If he had stepped closer, I'm sure I would have detected the stench of him; the stale smell of fags on his revolting, unbrushed teeth, and the rancid whiff of his foul body odour, clinging to his clogged and putrid pores due to a life-long allergy to soap and showers. His pallid, ageing complexion carried a sheen of sweat and grime. In his late-thirties he had stooped, making him appear like an old man even then. Now this bent figure of a man was near his sixties, a seemingly harmless pensioner shuffling around like a favourite old relative.

For years my nightmares had been haunted by this man: 'Captain' Eamonn Cooke, the famous Irish broadcaster and 'champion' of young people. That was his public persona, at least, and had been since the 1970s when he had first launched Radio Dublin, the popular pirate radio show. He had once been the darling of the airwaves: the people's choice, waving the flag for a modern and liberated young Ireland. But I knew his private persona all too well, and just one look into his face told me nothing had changed. For behind that cold, sinister stare lurked the same seething mass of hatred, perversion and depravity.

I had imagined this moment for a long, long time. Had fantasised about how I would one day take my revenge on him. Now I was face to face with my tormentor I stood rooted to the spot. Beads of sweat raced down my temples and collided with the tears that leaked involuntarily from my eyes. Here was the man who had viciously and remorselessly sexually abused me for four years, from when I was just a little girl of seven.

I had always thought I would try to gouge out his eyes or scratch the thinning skin across his cheeks until it bled. Given the chance, I had always wanted to pummel him with my fists until every ounce of strength was sapped from my body. I had always wished I could kick him so hard in the groin that he would double over in agony. But now the time had arrived I did absolutely nothing. Instead I trembled from head to foot. My mouth turned as dry as a desert, my lips locked together in silence. The only scream was in my head. Inside I raged, but outside I was frozen-faced.

I turned my attention from his stony, vacant gaze and saw

the faces of the children who stood close to his side. They could only have been about six or seven, the same age I had been when Cooke first began to paw at me and use my body for his own filthy and perverted sexual gratification. He had vandalised my body and left the indelible scars of his graffiti imprinted on my soul. Looking at those children was like holding a mirror to the child I was back then. When I stared into their eyes they looked dead. Like walking zombies, they clung on to the man I knew to be a monster. My heart filled with dread for them as he shuffled away from me with those two poor mites in tow.

I couldn't understand why I was still so afraid of an ageing pervert who had harmed me so long ago. I was a grown woman with four children of my own, and yet he still had the power to reduce me to feeling like a helpless child inside. I am not even sure he knew who I was that fateful day, the grown woman standing before him, shaking and crying. His only interest had been, and always would be, defenceless children. I, on the other hand, knew who he was and had no doubt at all that he was still an abuser.

He used to tell me I was his 'special girl' as he carried out his litany of unimaginable abuse, but feeling special was something that had escaped me for most of my adult life. I had been just one of the countless children he'd mercilessly defiled and then thrown on to the scrap heap when our innocent bodies became too mature to satisfy his twisted sexual desires.

I thought I had exorcised the ghosts of the past from my life, but in that moment I knew it was far from over. Eamonn Cooke had almost destroyed my life once. I knew I could never turn the clock back and erase the enormity of the crimes he'd committed against me, but I realised I might be able to stop him from harming other children.

This chance encounter heralded the start of a long and painful fight: my quest to bring justice and stop one of the most dangerous and persistent sexual predators of our time.

It all started a long time ago, as an innocent childhood adventure . . . but it became a lifelong nightmare. This is my story.

1

Nothing extraordinary happened in my life before I was abused. I grew up part of a normal, loving family in Ireland, which back then was a very different country from the one it is today. I was a typical child of my times. Born in 1967 to Liam and Kathleen Kennedy, I was the oldest of five siblings, two girls and three boys, in an era when children were seen and not heard.

I was a very happy child. My earliest memory dates from when I was about four. Mammy and Daddy took me and my baby sister Adrienne on a day out to Memorial Park, a recreation ground near our home. I remember it being a lovely hot sunny day and us playing by the duck pond. It wasn't a special occasion or anything but for some reason that day has stuck in my mind. I remember the flowers in the park and the bright blue sky and the warm contentment of being utterly happy.

Mammy tells me I was always happy as a child and was nicknamed 'Smiler' because I was constantly laughing and giggling. I was a chubby little thing with strawberry blonde, poker-straight hair and big blue eyes.

On the way home from the park that day we stopped for a treat at a grocer's store on our street that was run by a really kind man and his assistant. I just knew the man as Peter. It was a very old-fashioned place with a marble counter and shelves lined with jars of sweets. The shop was one of the first in our neighbourhood to get a fridge and for a long while after, a lot of the mammies would buy their milk and ask Peter to store it in the fridge for them, which he happily did until families could afford a fridge of their own. That was the sort of community we lived in, one where people still helped each other out whenever they could. These were simpler and less prosperous times, a world away from the materialism we know today.

Peter would always get a laugh out of me and I remember on this day Mammy said: 'Here, Peter, Siobhan has got a song for you.'

She lifted me up on to the counter and I sang my song, knowing that, as always, I would get a sweet at the end of it. I was easily bribed.

> *In the shade of an ole apple tree,*
> *Peter got stung by a bee,*
> *He sat on the grass,*
> *And a bee stung his arse,*
> *In the shade of an ole apple tree.*

By the time I had finished, everyone was in fits of laughter and old Peter thought it was brilliant. It was the sort of shop where everyone knew your business and the shopkeeper looked after everyone in the community. At Christmas-time he would give all the local smokers a few 'ciggies' as a present – and there were a lot of smokers back then. Most people weren't so well off either. If ever you were stuck for anything, Peter would help out until you could afford to pay him back.

Sometimes our local priest might call round unexpectedly on a Wednesday, two days before payday, so Mammy would send me running off to Peter's for a quarter of ham and a packet of chocolate Goldgrain biscuits. Tea and sandwiches would be served for the priest and I would sit salivating while Mammy gave me the evil eye – a silent warning not to touch the biscuits before the priest left. No sooner was he through the front gate than I dived in to finish them off.

I call these my unblemished years and remember them with great clarity and fondness. They were the days of Anglia cars and Grundig record players, *The Waltons* on TV and semolina pudding served with a dollop of jam. We were not a rich family but nor were we underprivileged. Like most working-class families of the day, we were not accustomed to luxuries, but we were comfortable enough and never went short.

I had a lovely clean home and we always had delicious home-cooked food. The menu rotated according to a strict routine with stew on Mondays, chops and potatoes on Tuesdays, fish on Wednesdays and Fridays, rissoles on Thursdays, and a lovely fry-up on Saturdays. Sundays were really special as we'd have a joint of bacon, corned beef or a chicken. Mammy served the meal with cabbage and potatoes and mushy peas, and it was the only day we had a dessert: jelly and ice cream. When we returned from Mass, the whole street smelled wonderful because dinner was dished up at the same time in every house along the road. This was because many of the dads would go to the pub until two-thirty when it shut for what was known as Holy Hour, so that was the time your daddy would be home and dinner was served. Chips were a rarity, so if we ever had a meal from the 'chipper' we were thrilled.

Daddy was a trained electrician and went off to work every morning while Mammy stayed home and worked hard too. We had a big granite step outside the front door and every day she scrubbed it so clean, she would say you could eat your dinner from it. She would always polish our brass doorknocker to perfection, too, and the dinner was always on the table in time for Daddy coming home from work. It was the same routine for all the women in our street.

My home life as a small child was idyllic. We had old sash windows in our house and, when it was really cold, you could hear the whistle of the wind through them. Every night Daddy would wrap me up in bed, all snug and cosy, and make up brilliant bedtime stories. My favourite was the tale of a bird that fell out of a nest and injured its wings. A little boy took him home to fix him and then set him free to be reunited with his mammy and daddy. Other times Daddy would sing 'Edelweiss' to me, and a song about the Angel Judy who came out of heaven to make me happy. If I had an earache or toothache, I would run to my daddy and lie on his chest. He said the heat would make the pain go away, and would sing me a song and stroke my hair until I fell asleep. I felt safe and protected and knew he would never harm me.

Saturday night was always the highlight of our life. That was bath-time. Like many people in Ireland back then, we didn't have constant hot water. My dad installed a gas water heater that had a pilot light. It made such a racket, I always giggled at the noise as I waited for the water to come out. Bath-time was always great fun. We would get dried in front of a huge open coal fire and then settle down to watch *Wanderly Wagon* on the TV. It was one of my favourite children's programmes, and followed human and puppet characters travelling around Ireland as well as around fictional magic lands, rescuing princesses and carrying out other good deeds. We would feast on Granby burgers, washed down with milk. If we weren't watching telly, we would sit down and play Snakes and Ladders as a family, or else Mammy and Daddy would tell us stories about when they were little. These never failed to make us roar with laughter and we had a hundred and one questions to ask them, driving them crazy in the process, but it was always great fun for all of us.

My parents were not overly strict but they were firm when they needed to be. We were taught discipline and respect, but that didn't stop us from pushing the boundaries of what we could get away with, as all kids do. When it came to anything slightly risqué, Daddy would always be the first to be embarrassed. We always knew if something slightly saucy came on to the television, even if we weren't watching it, because we would hear Daddy call out: 'Is there any football on the telly?' That was the cue to change channels and spare all our blushes!

It was the same when it came to our nightwear. Kids today jump into bed in their underwear or little else, whereas we were all trussed up like nuns to get a night's sleep. Once I walked down the stairs in my full-length nightie and Daddy shouted: 'Get your dressing gown on now!' It was not acceptable to be able to see your legs through your nightdress. I think every girl in Ireland must at one stage have possessed one of those disgusting quilted nylon dressing gowns that looked like you were wearing an old lady's lap blanket. They were also terrible fire hazards. As there was no central heating, we would stand by the coal fire wearing the things. I knew plenty of girls whose gowns caught fire. We look back and laugh now. It was all right to risk going up in flames, but God forbid anyone should see your legs through your nightie!

Even though I was a little livewire, I was taught right from wrong at an early age. Our family lived according to a strict moral framework. Mammy had a walnut cabinet in our house with three or four glass shelves in it. All sorts of ornaments adorned those shelves and they were my mammy's pride and joy. I remember one particular china trinket, about the size of a mug and in the shape of a toilet with a little wooden lid. I decided to pee in it and put it back on the shelf. (We had an outdoor toilet at the time and I was too cold to go outside.) I didn't tell anyone what I had done and as the weeks went by it began to smell. Mammy searched high and low to find out where the odour was coming from. It was driving her to distraction. Eventually she found it and demanded to know who had committed the crime. I only owned up when she promised that the culprit wouldn't be in trouble if they told the truth. It was my first lesson in being honest and has stayed with me throughout my life. My parents taught us that telling the truth was a good thing and that is something I have tried to hold dear all my life. I learned from an early age that telling lies not only hurts people's feelings, it also means you forfeit their trust.

Our family was one of the lucky few to have a car, which meant we were able to get away for holidays and take days out in the country. I loved to try and stick my hand out of the little window in the back. Daddy would drive us all to the mountains or the beach where we would happily play and have lemonade and crisps. Another favourite trip was to a place called the Hell Fire Club, which was up in the mountains, and Daddy would tell us we were going to see the devil there. We would get all excited and scared at the same time. My favourite holiday spot was Galway, which I believed was the most beautiful place on earth. We would go on holiday with my aunties and uncles and cousins, and I remember one particular trip when we packed into two cars and headed off for the Galway coast. What should have taken a few hours invariably took us about eight because we had to stop so many times for toilet breaks. Our cars were also incredibly unreliable and regularly stalled or overheated. We would have to sit on the roadside, waiting for the engine of one or other of the vehicles to cool down!

The very first place I went to in Galway was the beach and I still have the most magical memories of it. Compared to the east coast of Ireland where we lived, the Atlantic Ocean seemed angry and violent but its natural beauty and energy made a lasting impression on me, even as a small child. We spent our days in our swimming togs, messing about on the beach where the mammies sat on blankets dishing out sandwiches, which were soggy and filled with sand. The daddies, meanwhile, would go and relax over a pint in the pub or watch a football match on the television there. They were wonderfully carefree times.

I remember on another visit sitting on a high rock just looking at the waves crashing into the coastline. Even though the water was so turbulent and boisterous, the swell of it moving in and out made me feel serene inside.

Sometimes Daddy would take me fishing and would spin wonderful yarns about the history of all the places around us. He had a knack for conveying a sense of the past and I loved to listen. The Galway coastline was a fantastic contrast to the suburbs of Dublin city and always instilled a sense of calm in me. It definitely inspired my appreciation of Nature. When we ventured further into the countryside, I was struck by how remote and wild this area was. I always remember it being very hot and sunny on our holidays, but I felt it would be very bleak indeed in winter and was fascinated by that.

Like all kids, we sometimes got into trouble without really meaning any harm. We all went off to play one afternoon and came across a field crammed with haystacks. I had never seen anything like it before. We ran over to them without a second thought. We had a ball, jumping up and down on them and rolling around as we giggled our heads off. The next thing we heard the farmer's wife, roaring and screaming at us to get away. We'd acted as we did in innocent fun. We hadn't realised we were damaging her property, or the amount of work involved in creating a haystack.

On holiday, the whole extended family shared one large

luxurious house, with constant hot water and comfortable furnishings. On one occasion I got lost. We went out on a shopping trip for the afternoon and when it was time to go home everyone bundled into the two cars and drove off. What no one had realised was that I was still gazing through the window of a souvenir shop as they all hurtled off down the road. In the mayhem that was our normal family day out, not one person had noticed I was missing! When I turned around the cars were both gone and I was mortified. *How could they have left without me? Did they not notice I was missing?*

With that I indignantly marched off down the road to give them a piece of my mind. I hadn't realised it was a three-mile walk home, and that was a long way on my little legs. By the time I got there I was exhausted and slunk through the door with a sad face, expecting everyone to be frantic with worry over me. But even worse than leaving me behind was the fact that they still hadn't noticed I was missing. When Mammy realised what had happened she was horrified and I ended up getting lots of cuddles and treats for the rest of the day, so it was worth the walk home!

The highlight of our holiday was a day out to a place called Leisureland. By today's standards it was very basic, but it was a fun park for children with giant slides and pools. It was the Disneyland of its day, and when I returned to school I remember bragging to all my friends that I had been there.

Back in Dublin we had more simple leisure pursuits; we would go to the park to see the deer, go fishing, or else watch Daddy play football. He was quite a player in his time until injury forced him to give it up. On the way home, I would invariably fall asleep in the car, tired out but blissfully happy.

I was boisterous, content and bursting with life. Not for one moment did I ever imagine that the uneventful routine of my daily existence could change.

2

The neighbourhood I was born and brought up in was a working-class suburb of Dublin called Inchicore. It was a very ordinary and respectable place, typical of its time in Ireland. The small terraced houses were built in 1897 and were neat and sound dwellings. Sandwiched between two rows, at the back of the houses, was a cul-de-sac with garages and this is where we children would often play. All the kids in the area played out in the street together while their mammies cleaned and cooked at home and their daddies went out to work. Everyone thought it was perfectly safe. It was the normal practice of the day to let kids play outside as they were only ever within shouting distance of their own front door. If a mammy wanted a child, she would just holler their name and they would run home. So the kids had the run of the street and everyone played with each other outside. It was unheard of for children to play in each other's houses. It just wasn't allowed.

My life was very simple. Before I was old enough to start school, I would get up at the crack of dawn and go and knock for my friends in the street and then we would spend the whole day out playing. Mammy would always want to know where I was playing and who I was with, but we generally stayed nearby. She didn't check up on my whereabouts because she feared I was going to be abducted or interfered with – more because she wanted to know where I was for my dinner. We never had a big lunch. When we were out playing we would just pop back home for jam sandwiches or sardines on toast when we got hungry.

I got up to all sorts with a gang of kids who were about the same age as me. Sometimes it was simple games like skipping or playing with our dolls. Our favourite game was 'begs'. We would chalk out squares on the pavement and then fill old snuff tins with stones. If we couldn't afford chalk, we used yellow brick instead to mark the lines. Then you had to stand on one leg and kick the tins over the line. The neighbours hated this game because they said it made a mess but the rain always washed away the chalk marks.

A railway line ran behind our houses. There was a wall that blocked the track off, but it had a hole in it big enough to squeeze through so we would sneak on to the line and try to race the trains as they went by. We would play hide and seek, too, and there was an orchard nearby where we would get a 'bunt' over the wall and steal apples. One time, someone told on me to Mammy and, before I knew it, she was standing on the other side of the wall.

'Siobhan Kennedy, I know you are in there. Come out here now!' she roared at me. 'If you don't come out, you are in big trouble.'

I knew I had been caught red-handed, doing something I shouldn't, and the game was up. I crept back over the wall, with my tail between my legs, and she gave out to me something rotten. When she'd finished shouting, she explained that she was only mad at me because I could have hurt myself.

In my parents' eyes, the worst possible disgrace was if a neighbour knocked on the door to complain about their kids. You were in huge trouble if that happened, because they saw it as bringing shame on the family. It was an era when you were still expected to respect what any adult told you to do. If someone complained about me, I got the worst possible punishment by being banned from seeing my friends for two days.

I was a real chatterbox and naturally nosey and inquisitive. I was definitely one of the gang leaders and if we played 'knick knock' – where you knocked on a door and ran away – it was usually at my suggestion. We were not bad kids but we were always playing pranks and looking for new adventures to entertain ourselves.

Another favourite game was pretending to have a picnic. We used to collect wildflowers and weeds with yellow tops on them which we called 'eggs'. Stones were used for potatoes and our ice-lolly sticks were sausages. We would spread our blankets out and be in our element with our make-believe feast. Summer-time was always the most fun because we could play out the longest then. None of the kids could bring their friends into the house and so if the weather was too bad to play out, it was a nightmare for us. We would have to stay cooped up until it was mild enough to play outside with our friends.

In the autumn we would pick blackberries in Memorial

Park where we would also play hide and seek, more or less safely. Once I fell into a pond looking for frogs and had to be brought home soaking wet. Then there was the man who lived on our road who had an allotment plot on the park; we would walk up and buy fresh rhubarb and scallions off him, and called him Scallion Head because of this. It was all very innocent and meant in jest, though.

TV came into its own in the winter because you couldn't go out to play as much with your friends and were confined indoors on your parents' orders. As kids, we didn't care about the bad weather, we just wanted to get out and play.

Birthdays were always a good *craic* though, and whatever the time of year, the parties were great fun. When I look back, the presents we received were hilarious. You never got toys from your friends. Instead, you would get pencils, rubbers and copies (notebooks) — things that other mammies thought would be useful for a child and might save your family a bit of money. A birthday party was one of the rare occasions your friends were allowed in the house and it would be riot of games and laughter, with plenty of sweet bars and cakes.

When I was five, I went to school for the first time at the Model school in Inchicore. I remember getting dressed up in my new uniform and shiny shoes and feeling really important. I loved school from day one and was a good pupil. Mammy put my hair into two plaits which I hated, but I had to tie it up for school. School uniform was a kimono-style dress that I would wear with a poloneck jumper underneath.

I felt very big and grown up on my first day at school and

wasn't a bit afraid. I was really looking forward to it because I had seen all the other children going in and couldn't wait to get there myself. I can't remember anything that was said to me but I remember taking out my pencil and rubber, and the characteristic smell in that school which is still there – I think it came from the old floorboards, the wooden desks and the crusty inkwells. I clearly remember my first day in school because another girl did a poo in her pants and I thought it was hilarious. I stayed at the Model school until I made my First Holy Communion.

A lot of the social events in our house revolved around religious holidays, such as Christmas, Easter and St Patrick's Day. My favourite festival, like most children's, was Christmas, but not just because we got presents. I adored everything about it and it is still my favourite time of the year, perhaps because I associate it with people being jolly. I loved hearing stories about the baby Jesus – I thought it was the most magical thing I had ever heard – but I have to say I still preferred Santa Claus. In my own simple way, though, I knew that when Santa Claus came it meant the birth of the baby Jesus.

I remember the first Christmas when Mammy and Daddy explained to me about 'Santie' and how I had to go to bed early. I was really hyped up and excited and, instead of going to sleep, I sat up giggling. The next day, I was terrified of going downstairs too early in case Santa hadn't left. I knew that meant I wouldn't get any presents. Instead, I snuck into Mammy and Daddy's bedroom and asked if I could go down. They said no, and went down before me. It wasn't until years later that I realised they were busy switching on the Christmas tree lights and making everything nice for us kids.

My presents were quite simple by today's standards: teddy bears, dolls, prams, plastic tea sets, nurse's outfits, spinning tops and rocking cots, which, of course, I believed were all from Santa. I even got home-made gifts, including one year a cardboard dressing table. It was my pride and joy and I was thrilled with it.

Mass was obviously a very important part of Christmas too. As a family, we would go to the Oblate Church near our house, and the highlight for me was seeing the giant crib and its wax figures of Jesus, Mary and Joseph with all the farmyard animals. I loved the story of the Nativity and, as daft as it sounds today, for me it was practically as exciting as Disneyland as a spectacle. Pretty candles were lit everywhere and there were little waterfalls into which you could throw coins and make a wish. Pure magic. It was the first introduction I had to my religion, and from that moment on I loved hearing stories about Jesus. Christmas carols also hold special memories for me too.

There was a real sense of celebration in the town, and I have romantic memories of it being as picturesque as a scene from Dickens. Sparkling lights were strung in every shop and the festive atmosphere was almost overwhelming for a child. There would be Christmas songs on the radio as well as proper singsongs in our house. I remember every detail, down to the fresh turkey hanging by its neck on the back of our door and the smell of a succulent ham roasting in the oven. The aromas of Mammy's home cooking were mouth-watering and her Christmas puddings still the best I have tasted.

Christmas dinner was amazing. We would all sit round a big table decorated with balloons, crackers and holly. With the coal fires roaring, we would tuck into turkey and ham, roast potatoes, Brussels sprouts and stuffing. Pudding meant jelly and ice cream, trifle, or Christmas pudding with lashings of cream. There was plenty of food and plenty of laughter and joking – it was a real family affair. The adults would enjoy a drink, and for us kids there was cream soda and raspberryade from glass bottles. All day long there were crisps, sweets and nuts freely available, unlike other days of the year when they were strictly rationed treats.

We had a large family with lots of aunts and uncles and cousins, and so the children were all spoiled rotten at this time of year. We had two grandmas to visit on Christmas Day, which meant two lots of presents – heaven for a bunch of rowdy kids! But what I remember most was the sense of anticipation and excitement that I still enjoy with my own family today at Christmas.

Us kids always had a new rig out for special occasions; for Christmas it was white tights, black patent leather shoes, a little red skirt and a red and white polo-neck jumper. I only remember it snowing once, and I wore a white fake-fur coat with a little fake-fur muffler strung around my neck to keep my hands warm. All my friends and family would tell me how gorgeous I looked – and, of course, I believed them. The downside was the dreaded ribbons Mammy insisted on wrapping in my hair. The ribbons would come out for every special occasion, changing colour to reflect the event. Red for Christmas, of course. On St Patrick's Day, I would be dressed in green from head to toe with emerald ribbons to finish the look off. Worst of all was Easter, when we were trussed up in bright yellow clothing and ribbons, looking like demented chickens. The same rules applied to our jelly desserts – red for Christmas, green for Paddy's Day, and so on. It's funny when I look back on it, but I hated those ribbons at the time. The only compensation at Easter was all the lovely chocolate eggs we would get from the family.

Our treats were more restricted in those days. You couldn't just go to the fridge and take a bar of chocolate, like a lot of kids do today. There were no Chinese takeaways or any fast-food chains. The nearest we had was the chip shop that I knew as 'Missy's'. Sometimes my dad would come in on a Friday from work with a bit of fish and I would rob the batter from him. It was lovely! When I was slightly older, Mammy would send me round for three bags of what we called 'singles', which meant a bag of chips. The only problem was, I kept dipping into them on the way home and by the time I got back I only had two bags left! One day I went into 'Missy's' and she asked me if I kept eating the chips on the way home. I told her the truth and from that day on she would give me a free half-bag of chips for myself to eat on the way back. Unknown to me at the time, she did that for every kid in Inchicore if they went into her shop.

I was introduced to the Church by my parents. Like a lot of Catholics they believed that being a Christian was an important part of family life. In my early years, the Church represented a place of happiness for me. I learned all the Bible stories, and then when I was prepared to make my First Communion, I learned all the hymns too and about the meaning of the Holy Communion. I couldn't wait to get my beautiful white dress and remember thinking how much I loved God because he was such a lovely, good man. Innocence itself, I would tell Mammy and Daddy that I would never be afraid to die because God was up in heaven and I knew he would look after me. I also knew I would get to meet all my ancestors who had gone on before me. I imagined it as a beautiful place filled with flowers and sunshine. My parents were not the sort of people to dwell on tales of eternal damnation. They didn't go on about hell or anything like that, but they did explain the concept of the devil who tried to make you do bad things.

I loved the idea of angels floating around in heaven on delicate wings, spending their days doing good deeds and looking after people. The idea of having my own Angel Guardian was just amazing to me. Daddy would tell me that she was with me at all times to look after me. At night I would say three prayers with him. We started with the Our Father, followed by the Hail Mary, and the prayer to the Angel Guardian was always the last. Daddy would tell me that when I was awake the Angel Guardian sat on my shoulder but remained invisible. When I was asleep, she stood guard to protect me. It was just a lovely way to think of it all.

Mass could be a bit boring because I didn't always know what was going on, but it was a regular part of our lives and I went with my family anyway. It was only after I'd made my First Communion that I would sit up at the front of the Church and try to listen to every word the priest said.

Priests would often visit our house, as they did all the homes in the parish. I didn't really speak to the priests because, until I started school, it was left to Mammy and Daddy to explain religion to us. Daddy was the one who would tell me all the stories about Jesus, and I remember being as enthralled as if he'd been reading a bedtime story from one of my favourite books. I was mesmerised by tales of the life of Jesus. From an early age I had a strong sense of the love and safety our community's faith offered. Ireland in the 1970s was very much a society dominated by the Catholic Church and its clergy remained the most revered community leaders of the day; they were trusted implicitly and provided the moral compass by which we led our lives. In our sheltered and somewhat naive communities, drugs and armed robberies were virtually unheard of. Family life was much more innocent and simple compared to modern times. There was little or no public awareness of child sex abuse. It was certainly never reported on the news like it is today. Three decades ago it was unimaginable to most people that such appalling events even took place. The notion that a trusted 'man of the cloth' could abuse a child simply would not have been believed.

3

My childhood continued as normal until just after my seventh birthday in 1974, when Eamonn Cooke crept into my life. Up to this time he'd been a stranger to me. Even though he had lived in our street before I was born, I didn't know he existed. As a kid, I was only interested in the other children I played out with and so those were the families I mostly knew in the neighbourhood. I could never have imagined then the enormous impact his presence and actions would have on my life. But from the moment I first met him, my world changed forever.

Cooke was an outwardly unremarkable chap who lived with his wife, ten doors away from my home. To the outside world, he was just another working-class man, in his late-thirties, getting on with his life. But in fact Cooke was anything but ordinary or respectable. He was a dangerous and predatory paedophile who systematically abused children and had a reputation for violence.

Cooke had a radio scanner and would often listen in to the Garda frequencies. (In Ireland our police force is known as the Garda Síochána, which is Irish for 'Peace Guard'.)

Bizarrely, Cooke nicknamed himself 'Batman' or 'The Caped Crusader' because of the way he would find out about crimes through Garda radio and then turn up at the scene of the crime before the Gardaí even arrived. It was all very strange. The Garda had six radio frequencies and so dubbed Cooke Alpha Seven because he was the extra, unwanted man. They never really understood why he wanted to be at the scene of crimes. Perhaps it was part of his rebel nature or perhaps he was just trying to taunt the police by indicating he was always one step ahead of them. Whatever the reason, it certainly wasn't normal behaviour.

The most striking things about Eamonn Cooke were that he had a massive nose and he smoked strong untipped cigarettes. He also stank of BO and many years later, during his trial, admitted that he didn't believe in taking baths. He was dirty, dishevelled and smelly, always with a 'ciggie' hanging from his mouth. The man was like a walking ashtray. Cooke was short and quietly spoken, his thick, grey hair brushed to one side. He always seemed to wear the same navy or dark-coloured trousers and a shirt with its sleeves rolled up. I particularly remember how he loved his Jaguar cars, which he would drive around the streets of Dublin. Later on he would pick me up in a car like that and take me to his house.

By 1977, he would be a household name in Ireland when he took over a small pirate radio show already in existence. Radio Dublin was broadcast from his living room. In a short space of time it became a phenomenon. But when I first had the misfortune to meet him, he was just another outwardly ordinary bloke in our community.

I don't remember what led us to venture further afield the day I met Cooke, why we didn't just shelter from the rain at home. It started like any other day, when I told Mammy I would be playing out with some of my friends, and we fell upon Cooke's house by accident when we took shelter alongside his garage from a torrential downpour of rain.

We often played in the garages at the back of our houses which had little underground bunkers in them that we called 'pits'. They were just dugouts that were designed to allow a man to lie inside so as to examine a car from underneath.Sometimes the neighbourhood children used them to put on shows. The older kids would play the grown-ups and would ask us younger kids to play the children. If you got asked to be in the show, you were chuffed. We'd hide in the pit until it was our turn to be on the 'stage', then you would come on like a star, even though you would be stinking and covered in muck. Mammy knew I played in the garages and was used to me coming home filthy when I had been out – that was the way it was then. It's not that she liked me coming in with my clothes dirty, but play was a lot more rough and tumble in those days and I think most of the mammies expected their children to walk through the door wearing half a ton of muck! It still didn't stop them giving out to us, though.

The garages were fairly haphazard in the way they were laid out. Cooke's garage was the end one in a row of five. It was not attached to the houses by any man-made construction, but brambles and hedgerow from the house nearest his garage had grown over into an arch and attached themselves to the side of the building, forming a kind of tunnel. No one could see you from the main street if you went in or out of there.

One day, a group of us knocked at a friend's house to see if we could play in her garage, but there was no answer. It was belting down with rain and so we ran into the tunnel to take shelter. It was then that I noticed a little makeshift door. It wasn't even a real door – just a hole that had been cut into the dilapidated wooden door to Cooke's garage. It was just big enough for a child to fit through.

Being so nosey, the first thing I wanted was to go straight in there and see what was inside. It was very dark and damp and there was a heavy stench of oil and grease. To this day, if I step on a ferry or a ship and smell oil, I get a flashback that makes me feel violently sick and takes me right back to when I first entered Cooke's garage. Inside, it was crammed with all sorts of electrical equipment, such as televisions and radios, telephones and cables. We couldn't believe our luck! This was at a time before any of us had this sort of thing at home. We were all so excited, I remember we laughed and giggled as we pretended to be on the phone or the television. It was like walking into Aladdin's Cave for us.

We continued to go back to the garage to play as it seemed as if Cooke never used it and we hoped we wouldn't get caught. It was our new and exciting play den. It must have been weeks before we ran into him and I will never forget that day. One afternoon we were happily playing in there when all of a sudden we heard this voice.

'What are you doing in here, girls?' he said softly.

I froze with fear. In a split second we all made a run for it, trying to get out of the garage. We were petrified at being caught, but then he said: 'It's okay, girls, I was just asking what you were up to. You can carry on playing.'

We had all been expecting him to roar and growl at us, but he wasn't angry at all. It was such a relief because we had thought we were in big bother and instead he made us feel that it was okay for us to be there. He had not reacted in the way other grown-ups we knew would have. Given how strict the rule was that you were never to go into other people's homes, we would have expected to be run out of the garage and chased down the road, followed by a barrage of complaints to all our mammies. After that, Cooke's garage very quickly became a place where we were made to feel comfortable. We hadn't been invited in, but we hadn't been asked to leave either, and it was the turning point in so many of our lives.

Some of us carried on going back there to play. We wouldn't go every day; sometimes we would play by the trains or do something different, but it became a new place for us to venture to. From very early on, our trips there became our little secret. Our group varied in number but mostly it would be just a few of us. It was like being a member of some amazing secret club with an ideal hideaway, straight out of an Enid Blyton book.

The garage was a very messy place; there was a Jaguar parked in the middle of it and we used to play in the cramped space around it. The most exciting thing was all the broadcasting equipment. We didn't even have a telephone at home at the time, so to be allowed to play with all this stuff was beyond our wildest dreams. Some of the televisions were just empty shells. We could put our faces in the back and pretend we were TV stars. After a while we started taking our dollies down there so we could build them make-believe homes out of the spare broadcasting equipment. Cooke wasn't always there, but when he was he would quietly tinker away at something, and just let us get on and play. At first, when he was there, he hardly spoke to us. Over a period of weeks we all began to feel very much at home and comfortable in the garage, whether he was there or not. Unknown to us, we were slowly being drawn into his trap, like eager flies to a spider's web.

By that summer we were regular visitors to Cooke's garage and garden. Other than the days Mammy and Daddy took our family on holiday or on trips out to the country, I couldn't wait to join the secret garage gang. We wouldn't spend all day there, at the most a couple of hours at a time, but our trips to Cooke's garage or garden became part of our regular play routine, just like our picnics and playing by the train tracks. When I left Cooke's and returned home, little more went through my mind other than to wonder what was for dinner that night.

Cooke would also let us sit in his car, which we all loved, especially the boys and myself as I was a real tomboy. I can still recall the distinctive smell of the soft leather seats, a smell that still haunts my memory today. As the weeks rolled by, Cooke would talk to us a little bit more each time we saw him in the garage. It made us feel very important because in those days adults didn't give children that sort of attention. In our innocence, we just thought everything was grand and that this was an unusually nice man who was generous enough to let us play on his property.

Sesame Street was one of the most popular children's TV programmes at the time, and so after a while we nicknamed him the Cookie Monster, after one of the Muppets on the show. It was first coined as a term of endearment. Little did we know how sinister this nickname would grow to become in the months and years to follow.

Whenever I was in the garage, I would play with a lovely cream telephone which had become my favourite item there. I would pick it up and dial made-up phone numbers, having conversations with imaginary friends at the other end. Other times I would pretend to be a secretary or receptionist at work. I loved that phone. Sometimes I would even get my dollies to pretend to speak into it. One day, after we had been going to the garage for weeks, I went down there and the phone was gone. I looked for it and saw it had been put up on a high shelf that I couldn't reach. I tried to jump up and get it but it was no good.

'What are you looking for, little one?' a voice behind me said.

It was Cooke, standing so close I could feel his hot breath on my neck.

'My phone,' I answered.

'Don't worry,' he replied. 'Stand on this ledge and I'll lift you up to get it.'

In the 1970s in Ireland, little girls always wore dresses or skirts with slips or petticoats underneath them. Jeans or tracksuits were not part of our wardrobe, as they are for kids today. I can't even remember owning a pair of trousers.

That was the first time Cooke touched me. As he went to lift me up, he put his hands up my skirt and clasped them around my body. I didn't think anything of it because he'd helped me to get my phone and I was happy. But that was the way in which he subtly introduced me to being touched. The only men who had ever lifted me up before that were my dad or an uncle, and there was never anything untoward or sinister about that, so I had no reason to feel uncomfortable this time and carried on my merry way.

This gradual and subtle level of touching continued for quite a long time. On another occasion, I dropped my doll on the floor and Cooke came up behind me to pick it up. Again his hand went up my skirt. I barely acknowledged it, and anyway he was also doing the same thing to some of the other girls in the garage, so it didn't seem out of the ordinary or as if he was singling me out in any way. Other times he would just come up behind me and stand so close I could hear his heavy breathing, but we were all so young and innocent, it didn't occur to us that this wasn't normal behaviour.

None of us ever told our mammies or daddies we were playing in the garage. I was still only seven and concerned purely with having fun with my friends, blissfully unaware of the horrors that Cooke was slowly paving his way to. We all knew we were not allowed in other people's homes, and he would have known this also. If we had told anyone our parents would have stopped us playing in our favourite place, which was the last thing we wanted, and so it remained a secret from the beginning.

When I came home really filthy, covered in oil or dirt, Mammy would roar, 'Would you look at the state of you — how in heaven's name could you get so dirty?'

I would just lie and say we had been playing down at a friend's garage, and she had no reason to disbelieve me. In my mind, one garage was the same as the next.

Cooke also ensured our silence by subtly planting ideas into our gullible minds. In his quiet voice, he would say, 'If your parents knew you were here, they might be giving out to me for letting you play with all this stuff.'

He was putting into our minds the suggestion that we shouldn't tell our families because then they would stop us from visiting him. His secret grooming of us had begun. Already we believed that the blame for our being in Cooke's garage was ours alone. He had created a secret, between him and us, and in doing so had shifted the onus of responsibility and guilt from himself and on to the shoulders of innocent children – without so much as uttering a single threat. These would come later. For now, we were happy to go along with the Cookie Monster and his subtle tactics. Cooke would prove himself a master of manipulation. I certainly didn't feel at all threatened by him then. I just thought he was a nice, quietly spoken man who let us play in his garage because he had no children of his own. He would even talk to us about his wife and other adults, something your own mammy and daddy would never do, and this was taken as a great privilege.

Weeks went by while we continued to play in the garage. One day a gang of us went down there and Cooke was playing around with some projector screens. He told us he was fixing them so that he could use them with a new camera. He then said he wanted to take some pictures of us, film us all dancing. He said we would have to go into the garden because he needed sunlight to film us by. Then he said he would put the film on a giant screen in his house and we could watch ourselves like movie stars. I was so excited. We all were. None of us had ever done anything like this before. The idea of seeing ourselves on television was out of this world.

We went into the garden and he asked us all to dance for him. He then asked us to pull up our skirts and dresses, which we gleefully did, not having any sense of this being inappropriate because of our young age. I remember one particular girl who I will call Janet. She had on black knickers and I had never seen the like before. I remember thinking it would be handy to have some because my mammy was always giving out to me about my knickers being dirty from playing in the mud and grime.

I was wearing my favourite outfit that day. It was a cerise, pink and purple Crimplene dress, with a lace collar. I thought I looked gorgeous in it and remember pulling my dress up no end and laughing my head off, thinking what a great time we were all having.

Throughout the filming, Cooke would tell us what to do. He would ask us to kick our legs up or pull our dresses higher. We just squealed with delight because we thought this was the best game we had ever played. There was a line of us and we ended up doing a dance, just like the Can-can, as Cooke filmed us. For us kids it had been a fantastic day, filled with fun and laughter. We were too young and naive to understand it was all part of his sick perversion. That was it for that day. Once he'd finished filming we all went home happy, and carefree.

We didn't get to see the film as soon as we'd hoped. After that day, he kept asking us to go into his house to watch the movie of our dancing. But when we got inside, he would make excuses that the film wasn't quite ready or the camera wasn't working properly. In all honesty, my friends and I didn't care a hoot. Now, the mere fact that we were allowed in his house was far more exciting and unusual. This was even *better* than the garage and garden, and we were astonished that he would let us have the run of the place. It was a free-for-all and we were allowed to run wild. There were no boundaries or limits to what we could do there, in direct contrast to our behaviour in our own homes.

Little did we realise that we had seamlessly slipped into a new routine of playing inside the house, a place we knew really was forbidden, and yet we didn't worry about it. To us it was Utopia. The reality was that Cooke had moved on to the next stage of his grooming and drawn us one step further into his lair.

4

Cooke continued to win our confidence before he dared to step up the level of abuse. We rarely went into his house if his wife was around. If we were in the garage sometimes he would tell us we couldn't go into the garden – always for some different reason – and looking back, I believe that was when his wife was in the house. She would have been able to look out of the window and see us in the garden. We certainly were never brave enough to go into the garden unless he invited us to do so.

When his wife was out, we would be allowed back into the house to play to our hearts' content. I remember the layout really well, though I don't recall much about the décor. I just knew that it wasn't like my mammy and daddy's house. It was a bit grotty and untidy, and I also remember it seemed old-fashioned and uncared for. I don't think I would really have thought to judge a house as dirty, or not at that age, but Cooke's house certainly didn't have the lovely fresh smell of my own. What was impossible to escape was the stench of cigarette smoke and the memory of it still taunts me today. The pungent overwhelming smell clung to everything in that house. He was always a heavy smoker, but Mammy was unlikely to detect the smell of his cigarette smoke on my clothes as she smoked herself.

There were three rooms downstairs: a kitchen at the back, a middle room, and a living room at the front with a long hallway leading from it. In the middle room was a live phone and, to our amazement, Cooke even let us use that when we went in the house. We didn't know any phone numbers, so we would just pick up the receiver and dial at random to make some stupid call. We would get through to an unsuspecting adult and say, 'Hello, this is Mary, where's Joseph?' if it was a woman who answered, and if a man picked up, he would get, 'How's your baldy wife?' I remember once, one of the lads got through to a woman and shouted, 'How's your hairy beard, missus?' before slamming down the phone in fits of giggles. They were naughty, childish pranks which we knew we could get into big trouble for, ensuring we kept our little play den secret from the outside world.

Cooke also had a piano in his house. Not even that was off limits to us. All the kids loved the piano and we would try and bash out tunes on it, which must have sounded horrendous given that none of us knew how to play the thing.

Cooke was by now frequently putting his hand up my skirt, so much so that it seemed a normal thing for him to do. Gradually his contact with me began to intensify, but not so fast that I became alarmed and backed off. One day, I was playing by the piano when he came up close behind me. I felt something touching my back. When I turned around, I saw the ugliest and most surprising thing. My immediate reaction was just to laugh. What he had on full display was his erection. It was the first time he did this, and of course I didn't have a clue what it was; I only knew I had never seen my dad or any of my uncles like this.

'What's that?' I asked, in all innocence.

'Ah, that's just another part of the body, like a hand or a leg,' he replied. 'Do you want to touch it?'

I pulled back and said no, because I thought it was a scary-looking thing and it repulsed me. I was confused, though I don't recall feeling physically threatened by what Cooke was doing.

'You don't have to be afraid of it, it won't bite,' he tried to reassure me in a hushed tone.

After some hesitation, I touched it quickly then moved away as fast as I could. With that, Cooke walked off. He didn't even zip up his trousers and this gradual introduction of his partial nudity was how he continued to condition us to his perverted behaviour, carefully grooming us for more serious abuse. That day I remember I carried on playing in the house for a while, not at all put off by his strange behaviour, before I went home for my dinner as usual.

Cooke didn't take unnecessary risks. His acts were calculated and cautious. He didn't repeat anything like that with me for some weeks, obviously not wanting to scare me off. But the sustained physical abuse that I was to suffer in that house was already in motion, and with each cautious step forward he took care to make his behaviour appear normal. He began to touch me more. His hands going up my dress had become a normal occurrence for me. Now he began to rub my backside too and would moan softly.

In good weather we could be in that house three times a week, for a couple of hours at a time, staying there until we decided we fancied playing a different game elsewhere. We would never go back twice in one day. As the winter drew in, we went to Cooke's much less because we were not allowed out as much when it was cold and dark. We couldn't protest about it, though, as it had to remain secret that we played at the house. But there were compensations to the winter weather. At weekends at home, I would be allowed to stay up later to watch *Hawaii Five-O* on television.

I was still outwardly a happy and untroubled child. I behaved normally, and showed no signs of trauma or distress. I had absolutely no idea that what Cooke had been doing to me was wrong. I just had this secret world with my friends that my family knew nothing about. For some reason none of it seemed strange to me. I guess it all just felt like one big game and, after all, Cooke wasn't only touching me. It was happening to some of the other children, too, and none of them appeared to think it odd either.

Christmas came and went. As far as I remember, it was the happy and joyous occasion it always was. Then, at some point during the second year of visiting Cooke's house, he introduced something new. He started to move his hands to the front of my underwear. I remember feeling very strange about this, it felt less comfortable, but I didn't stop him because I didn't know it was wrong. Anyway, no sooner had he started than he would stop, so there was little time for me even to worry about it. By this stage, I trusted Cooke as he had never harmed me and his behaviour had always been consistent. After the first incident of this he adopted the same pattern as before, leaving me alone for a while and moving on to another child in the house. It was like he had us on a rota, all slowly being groomed at the same time, while he had a continuous supply of children to feed his dark desires.

It wasn't just children from our neighbourhood in the house. There were others I didn't know who would just appear out of nowhere and then go away again. There had been no big treats or bribes introduced at this stage, as all the kids were still easily captivated by the phones, cameras and televisions. Even being inside the house remained a novelty for us. Cooke continued to touch me in this new way and eventually, as his behaviour went on, I accepted that as 'normal' too.

Every time Cooke wanted to escalate his abuse, he would deal a new card from his box of tricks, to keep us interested and keen to stay in the house. Before long we would arrive to find biscuits or sweets or even a bit of fruit waiting for us. Of course, these treats delighted us.

On one occasion I was playing the piano. I was accustomed by now to him touching me between the legs, but on this occasion I felt something different. Cooke had turned me around in my seat and placed his erection between my legs instead. It completely took me by surprise as he had never done this before. I jumped up in shock.

'What are you doing?' I queried.

'Ah, I was just messing about, seeing what it would be like to do this, because it feels very nice. This is what people who like each other do. And if you like me, and I like you, then you won't mind. Do you mind?'

'No,' I replied, because he had made it seem so logical and

normal. The initial shock of his actions had subsided. Cooke had moved on another stage with his grooming for abuse.

It's hard looking back to explain why I didn't run away, but the abuse had been introduced so gradually that I wasn't frightened of him. He was just this friendly, quiet man down the road who let us play in his house. I didn't expect the same behaviour from this man as I expected from the other men in my life, so that what he did never really shocked me. I expected my dad to love me, to teach me, and take care of me when I was sick; I expected neighbours to give out to me if I was naughty. But Cooke was different from the norm, and his careful grooming had trained me to see him and his behaviour very differently. He hadn't created an atmosphere of fear or intimidation and I didn't understand the nature of the acts he was committing. I had no adult values of right and wrong in sex — I didn't even know what sex was so I had nothing to compare or measure his behaviour against. I simply trusted this adult who had befriended me.

Rarely did our parents ask us where we had been playing out during the day. It would never have crossed their minds that we may have been in some kind of danger from a man like Cooke, and furthermore they had no idea we were in and out of his house because it had remained a secret. Sometimes, in the winter, if the weather was bad we would sneak out, saying we were going to a friend's garage, but really we were going down to Cooke's. As well as the broadcasting equipment, we would play with his dog which all the kids loved. I'll never forget the time he showed us the litter of puppies his dog had given birth to. They were so tiny and adorable and everyone wanted to see and hold them. He let us all name a puppy of our own and we were thrilled. It was just another way of enticing us to go back to the house. It also provided him an excuse to give his wife for allowing us children into their home.

Incredible as it sounds, I still felt I was living a normal and happy life. I truly didn't appreciate that something bad was happening to me. There was one difference, though, and it wasn't until I was older that I realised its significance. Where once I would go and lie on my dad's chest if I had a headache or toothache, I had stopped doing that after Cooke began abusing me. I couldn't understand it as a child, but as an adult I began to recognise that he had taken away the feeling of safety I had always enjoyed with my dad. I had seen Cooke's whole anatomy, his bare perverted desire, and unknown to me that had changed my subconscious and the way I behaved towards the men in my home life. Cooke had ripped away that loving innocence I'd shared with my father and I would never be able to get that back. He had already had a profound and damaging effect on my life, even though I didn't realise it at the time. This became one of the most upsetting aspects of his abuse -- that he had tarnished the perfect childhood innocence of my relationship with my dad.

The more relaxed we became in Cooke's house, the easier it became for him to abuse us. There would be ice cream and sweets, biscuits and crisps, which he would allow us to enjoy at will and this would tempt us back time and again. His wife would often spend periods of days or weeks away from home and that made it easier for Cooke to abuse us without restraint. There was a small room upstairs that would usually remain locked. It was filled with television screens and monitors and one day he went in there and took out a collection of pornographic calendars. It was soft pornography. The pictures showed naked ladies with their 'diddies' out — that's what we would call breasts back then. I remember being fascinated by the photos because the girls were so pretty and they had long blonde hair. I would say to Cooke that I hoped I looked like the women in the pictures when I grew up. He said that one day my diddies would look like theirs. He would touch himself in front of me while I looked at the pictures. This was normal behaviour for him which did not, by this stage, appear strange to me as I didn't expect anything different.

One day, he finally announced that the film of us dancing was ready to watch. He said he had set the film screen up in his bedroom so we could all see it together. This is how he got us into the room with him for the first time. All the kids thought it was brilliant. We scrambled on to the big double bed and were allowed to jump up and down. We laughed so much, holding hands and letting ourselves fall all over the place. It was such a novelty to play rowdily on a bed because that was totally taboo in our own homes. Then, when we watched the film and saw ourselves dancing in Cooke's garden, we squealed with delight, trying to suss out which one of us had kicked their legs the highest. It all seemed astonishing to us because we had never seen anything like it before. We felt like movie stars.

After that first showing of the film, we would go to Cooke's and ask him to show us the movie time after time. We were so excited at seeing ourselves as little dancing divas, we wanted to watch it again and again and again. And every time we watched the film, it meant we had to go back into Cooke's bedroom. He said he had to set the screen up there, even though he could clearly have installed it downstairs, but this was his ploy to get us used to going into the bedroom. We didn't question it because we were only interested in seeing the film and didn't care where that happened.

His bedroom was very basic and simple. I just remember a bed with the head propped against a wall, a chair and a wardrobe. For some reason, the sheets on the bed always stick in my mind although I can't remember what the rest of the bed covers looked like. To me the bedroom was just like the rest of his house – shabby, scruffy and neglected, but still somewhere that we could do whatever we liked.

Cooke began to touch us regularly in the bedroom and it quickly became a normal feature of his repertoire of abuse. Still it had not dawned on me that this was wrong. I can only speak for myself, but I imagine the other children who were abused by him accepted it in the same way. None of us ever spoke to each other about it when we were not in the house.

After almost two years of our visiting the house, Cooke stepped up his sexual assaults once more. He began to abuse children in pairs, which was to become a pattern of his behaviour. If a group of children were playing in the house, he would take two of them to the bedroom. I'm sure it is hard for anyone to understand, but the abuse was so gradual that I was still comfortable around him. To our unquestioning minds, he had made his grotesque behaviour seem the norm.

I remember Cooke taking me and one other girl into his bedroom. He lifted both of us up at the same time, a child under each arm, and put us on his bed. Then he took our clothes off. The two of us were giggling away because we didn't know what was going on, he made it all seem such a game. It was cold and so we got under the blankets to warm up. Then Cooke took his clothes off too and got in the bed with us. He placed himself in between the two of us girls and showed us ciné-camera films of other children. This became a regular event. Tucked up in his bed, we would watch films of all these young girls walking past the school, which was on the opposite side of the road from the row of houses where I lived. They were all different ages, but I don't remember seeing any girls older than teenagers. All this time, he was also constantly asking me to bring more of my friends to his house. This was during a period that his wife was away. He would tell us that she was on her holidays.

While Cooke entertained us two girls with films or pictures, he would place his erection between my legs to arouse himself. I knew it felt strange, but because he had not penetrated me, it was not painful. I wasn't shocked because I had seen Cooke naked so many times by now that it had become a normal occurrence. The biggest shock for me remained the first time I had seen his nudity on the day I sat at the piano. I had also seen him naked with other children. When he was downstairs, he never took his trousers off but would walk around with his zipper undone and his erection sticking out. He wandered from child to child like this, as if it was the most normal thing in the world. The Cookie Monster lived to abuse children. Once or twice, I remember his trousers went down to his knees but his shirt and jacket remained on and he would puff on his cigarette at the same time as violating his victims. He never wore underpants, and this became a crucial piece of evidence at his later trials.

5

Cooke's tactics and behaviour changed once he started abusing me and my friends in his bedroom. For the first time, he introduced money as an incentive. Children in those days were rarely given money, apart from on very special occasions like a birthday or a First Holy Communion day. You might get a few pence if you ran an errand for a neighbour or a relative, but by and large the kids growing up in our neighbourhood didn't have anything like pocket money. So it was an effective enticement when Cooke began to give money to the children he abused in the bedroom. It would start with five pence and then go up to ten pence or even fifteen or twenty pence. In the context of the era, this was amazing.

But Cooke's depravity and manipulation knew no bounds. Instead of just giving money to us, he deliberately gave us differing amounts as a way of setting us in competition against each other. For example, if I was in the bed with Cooke and another girl, he might give me ten pence but give the other child twenty. When we got outside we two children would compare our spoils and you would feel annoyed if you got less money than your friend had. It also set you thinking that Cooke preferred the other girl to you. On the next occasion, he would turn it on its head and give me more money than the other girl. We began to compete against each other, trying harder to please him by doing the things he asked us. All children seek the approval of their elders and I was no different. I didn't know if Cooke's behaviour was good or bad, right or wrong. It was just something I had grown used to. The money he gave us was another way of making us more receptive to the escalating abuse he was to inflict on us. If you ended up with the lesser amount, you went away feeling inadequate. I would ask him why my friend got more money than me.

'Ah, well, she was better than you today,' he often replied.

When I quizzed him as to what he meant about being better, he would say, 'She let me touch her more than you did.'

He never used words to describe body parts and there was never any kissing. Everything he did was purely for his own sexual gratification. He would cup his hands around my bare chest, but I was too little to have a bust or any development at all. I particularly hated it when he pulled me close to his chest because his body smelled so awful. Sometimes I think I can still smell his BO and it makes me retch to the pit of my stomach. By forcing us to compete against each other, he could test how far he could go with us. It was a sickening and despicable manoeuvre to use on innocent children.

I loved getting the money and so did the other kids in the house, but in the end we got so much of it, we didn't know how to spend it. This was a significant aspect of Cooke's grooming. He knew we couldn't tell our parents about the money and that guaranteed our secrecy. I didn't know what to do with mine. I couldn't take it home because Mammy and Daddy would have said, 'Where the feck did you get the money from?'

I remember feeling more anxious that my parents would think I had stolen the money from them than I was about them discovering the truth. So I spent it all on sweets and little bits of stationery, which I hid at home under my bed. I bought Ice Pops, coke, crisps, pencils, rubbers, chocolate and notepads – anything, just so I could get rid of it. I would also spend it on other kids who hadn't got any money from Cooke. One girl was abused on the day she made her First Holy Communion while she was still in her lacy white dress. She told me many years later that Cooke paid her money that day and she hid the coins in one of her socks and hopped all the way home so that her parents didn't hear them jingling. The ridiculous thing is, I didn't feel guilty over what he was doing to me. I just felt guilt because I knew I was not supposed to accept money from people and that was enough to keep me silent, just as he had anticipated.

When Cooke's abuse progressed to him performing oral sex on me in his bed, the money I received went up again. If I went home with loads of sweets, I would just tell Mammy that one of the children in our group had given them to me. On many occasions, he performed oral sex on me and another girl in the bed at the same time. Once he was finished with me, he would start on the other girl.

Afterwards, he would say, 'Now, which one of you enjoyed that the best?' We didn't respond by speaking to him but giggled in our innocence and carried on playing.

One day, I was sitting on the bed while another girl was sitting in a chair in his bedroom. Cooke walked over, lifted her legs and began the same awful act on her. My response was nothing to do with the terrible abuse he had just inflicted – instead, I remember being upset because he had never abused me on the chair before. I was put out because he had only ever done it to me when I was in the bed, and because of the extreme sense of competition he'd instilled in us, I assumed it was because he liked her better than me. That was what hurt me most.

It was also the first time I had really been able to clearly see what he was doing. Prior to this incident, oral sex had taken place under the covers of his bed. For some reason, I remember it suddenly occurring to me that what he was doing didn't look right. Questions were slowly creeping into my head and, although I was jealous that Cooke did seem to be giving the other girl special treatment, I felt relieved too. From where I sat on the bed, I realised that what I was watching wasn't something I wanted to happen to me. It was a very childlike and simple response to something so shocking, but I couldn't really understand why I felt this way. I can't say it was shame I felt – that didn't come until many years later – but perhaps, for the first time, there was a sense of embarrassment welling in my subconscious. But this growing sense of unease made no difference. His abuse of me continued.

One of the worst things I remember about the oral sex was that the stubble on his chin would scratch the skin on my legs, and I hated that. The truly vile act he had carried out was dismissed by my innocent mind while the discomfort inflicted by his facial hair became the focus of my attention. I still didn't know that what Cooke was doing was wrong. He behaved as if it was normal so I had no reason to think otherwise. He would also get me and another girl to dance for him and rub his back while he was touching us.

I remember one time being in bed beside him. I was lying on my side and he was abusing me.

'Where do babies come from?' I asked.

'Something like what we are doing now,' he said.

My baby brother had been born by now and I got really spooked for the first time. He reassured me that I was not going to have a baby.

In most cases, the physical acts Cooke carried out on me are too appalling to describe. They have haunted my memories since childhood but it was not until I was an adult that I truly understood what a sick individual he was.

The rest of my life continued as normal. To the outside world and my parents I was no different from any other happy, carefree child. I was getting good reports from school, and I was neither disruptive nor outwardly troubled in class or at home. After I made my First Holy Communion, I moved to the Basin Lane School in St James Street. It was a bus journey away and I was miserable there at first because I missed my old school friends, but Basin Lane was handy for Mammy because one of my aunts lived in the same road. To my surprise, as I'd always been popular at my old school, I was bullied at first at this new one. I think it was because, not knowing a soul, I was uncharacteristically quiet, and being the new girl I made an easy target.

There were always little fights breaking out in the playground and one time the ringleader of this gang of girls started on me and said she would see me for a scrap in the school yard. She had no idea I was such a tomboy, though, and could look after myself, because I had seemed so timid in class. After school that day I went outside to meet her and a chant went up: 'Milly up, cha, cha, cha, milly up, cha, cha, cha.'

That was the signal that a fight was about to start. Before I knew it, loads of kids started buzzing round us like bees round a hive.

We started to fight and I must have pulled clumps out of this girl's lovely blonde hair. I was stronger and tougher than her, and by the time a nun pulled us apart it was evident that I was the winner. From that day on, I never looked back at that school. I suddenly had loads of girls who wanted to be my friend and I finally had a sense of fitting in. I became very much what we called a 'Basin Lane girl' and in the end I loved going to school.

After I had been there a while, I remember my dad came into class one day and said I had to go home early. I was about eight years old. Dad had tears rolling down his face and as we walked away from the school he told me that my grandma, his mother, had died. He said she had gone to heaven, and while I didn't really understand why, I knew she had gone to be with God. I was too young to attend her funeral but I remember feeling so sad for my dad because I thought it was terrible he would never see his mammy again. It upset me so much to hear him crying.

'Don't worry, Dad, you will see your mammy when you

go to heaven,' I tried to reassure him. Then I asked, 'Can Gran see us from heaven, Daddy?'

He told me that she could and that she would be looking down on us to protect us. Little did he realise how major an impact knowing this would have on me.

As time went on, I started to question Cooke's behaviour more and more. I had always been taught that God could see everything, but now I had the added notion that my grandma could see everything too. I remember being in Cooke's bed and feeling uncomfortable and scared that my grandma could see what he was doing to me. My immediate fear was that somehow she would be able to tell my dad.

A Wimpy Bar had opened up in Inchicore by this time, and it gave Cooke another method by which he could keep us sweet. I was on my own one day at his house when he said he was taking me for a burger. I got into his car and he told me to duck down in the seat until we got past my house and to the end of the road. He bought me a burger and chips and a fizzy Cola. It was a huge treat for me as it was the first time I'd ever had a fast-food meal in a burger bar. I remember his abuse of me was becoming relentless and increasingly scary by this time, so a treat like this was an effective way of making me feel there was some sense of payback and would distract me from thoughts of what had happened in his bedroom earlier during the afternoon.

When he took me home, he said, 'I don't think your mammy and daddy would be happy, now, if they knew you were in the Wimpy – you might get into trouble if they found out.'

He was so audacious! Once again he placed the burden of

guilt on to me, suggesting that *I* would be in trouble instead of him.

He persisted in asking me to bring other friends to his house and one day I gave in and decided I would. I had a friend from school who didn't normally play out in our neighbourhood so I asked if she wanted to see where I played. I took her down to Cooke's and we had only been there for a short while before he exposed himself to her.

She didn't go ballistic. Instead, she just blurted out, 'Oh my God, that's his mickey!'

My only response was, 'So?'

I had never heard the term 'mickey' before and certainly wasn't embarrassed by Cooke's behaviour. In some ways this incident could have posed an uncharacteristic risk for him, behaving the way he did to a girl with whom he was unfamiliar. But given the times we lived in, I believe he thought he could get away with anything. Looking back, he clearly thought no one would take the word of a school kid against his because at that stage no one suspected what a monster he was. On top of that, as I found out many years later, his need for fresh victims was far stronger than his fear of the law.

When I returned to school, this girl told everyone in the class, 'Siobhan Kennedy has a man in her road and he showed us his mickey.'

Once again, I just shrugged it off as nothing, but I never took any more girls from my school down to his house. I couldn't understand why she was shocked when I felt no embarrassment because I was so used to seeing Cooke naked all the time. When I look back at this incident, I can see the awful perversion of bringing a child to the stage where she doesn't think it strange or odd for a grown man to be naked or touching her.

Things dramatically changed for me when Cooke's physical abuse began to hurt me. On one occasion when he was rubbing his erection inside my legs, he tried to penetrate me for the first time. I cried out in pain, rigid with shock. He tried again but in the end gave up because I was so upset. It felt like a sharp dart of pain throughout my body. That is the only way I can describe it. He had never inflicted physical pain on me before. I didn't feel afraid but something just told me, for the first time, that what he was trying to do was very wrong. I was on my own with him when this incident happened and clueless as to what he had tried to do. When he saw me wincing he stopped quickly. He said he was sorry and that it was 'an accident'. Looking back, he must have been worried that he had overstepped the mark in a way that might compromise his secret. He certainly never felt any remorse for his actions.

In my ignorance I accepted his explanation and as a result was not too afraid to visit his house again. His grooming of me over the years meant that he now performed oral sex on me regularly and I didn't know what he was doing. It's not hard to see, therefore, how I accepted his explanation that attempting to have full sex with me was an accident.

As an adult, I look back on this incident with sheer horror. When I went to give my statement to the Garda years later, I realised what he had tried to do to me then and was filled with pure hatred for him.

My reaction to the incident spooked Cooke enough for him to give me the largest amount of money I had received from him so far. He gave me an Irish pound note, which absolutely blew me away. I had never had that much money before in my life, but it also scared me witless. How was I going to get rid of it? It was clearly intended as hush money as well as an inducement for me to continue going to his house.

I hatched a plan to organise a picnic for me and the girls so I could spend all the money. I organised a meeting with my gang, and when I told them how much money Cooke had given me they were flabbergasted. I confided that I got the money after he had an accident and hurt me. One of the other girls told me that Cooke had also had 'an accident' with her but she had not received as much money. Off we went to the sweet shop without thinking anything more of it. We bought Club lemon drinks, sweets, crisps, chocolate, chewies, jellies and biscuits – anything to spend the cash. Then we took our stash and went to a secret hideaway of ours to feast on the picnic. It was by no means a safe place to go but we had always gone there when we didn't want to be seen by anyone. Our picnic was held underneath the railway bridge in a hole in the brickwork. It was like a little cave away from the prying eyes of our parents. We went home with bellies swollen like poisoned pups because we had eaten and drunk so much. It was the first and last time I ever received a pound note from Cooke.

This short period of time when his abuse of me suddenly escalated is difficult for me to talk about because it brought so much shame into my adult life. At the time I was still drawn to visit his house even though I was clearly becoming confused. The incentives he gave me, and the freedom in the house, were still enough to lure me back time and again because that's how effectively he had groomed me. What happened in his bedroom that day, which he passed off as 'an accident', was one of the most frightening examples of his power over me and the extent to which he would go in order to fulfil his disgusting and perverted desires. But it didn't stop there.

A short while later, I was on my own in his bedroom when he came in and offered me a banana to eat. I was delighted because fruit was kind of scarce for us at the time. It was a very strange experience because while I remember him coming into the bedroom and me then eating the fruit, I can't recall anything of what happened next. So much of what Cooke did to me is vividly imprinted on my memory to this day, that I'm certain that on this occasion I was drugged. I didn't knowingly take any tablets, but I can never be sure that he didn't put something into that banana.

The next thing I can remember is waking up in his bed and realising that I didn't know what had just happened. I was lying on the side of the bed, groggy and disorientated. I felt really sick and poorly. More than anything, I remember feeling frightened because it was the first time I had ever woken up in any environment other than my own home, or at least woken up to find my family were nowhere nearby. I know I can't have been asleep for more than an hour because it was late in the day and Cooke would have known I had to be home for my dinner. Worse still, I felt very uncomfortable.

I suddenly felt like I wanted to go to the toilet and my bottom was very sore.

Then I saw blood on the sheets. I was horrified and asked Cooke where it had come from. He said he had cut himself shaving, but I knew it couldn't be that because it was right where I had been sitting. I didn't know what to think back then, but many years later it dawned on me that something very terrible happened that day. Today I am certain that he drugged me in an attempt to rape me anally while I was unconscious.

This experience sickens me so much I have never been able to speak publicly about it before. I couldn't even include it in my adult statement to the Garda because even now it makes me feel dirty and embarrassed. When it happened I didn't feel dirty as I was too young to realise the significance of the assault. At Cooke's criminal trial, I met two more of his victims who had been through the very same experience some years after me and realised then that it was not a one off – it was the very worst level of his abuse. His depravity knew no bounds.

I confessed to one of the victims I met at the trial that I had not felt able to say everything in my police statement because I had felt so much shame at some of what had happened to me. I confided that, at that stage, I had not even been able to tell my own husband. She asked if I would share what letter the act began with and I said 'b'. She asked if he had buggered me and I said I wasn't sure but believed he had certainly attempted to. Then, to my horror, it came up again with another of the victims who said, 'Oh my god, he told me the blood on the sheets was tomato sauce.'

Mercifully, I had remained asleep throughout the whole incident.

That was probably the most severe assault on me, but through a misplaced sense of shame and embarrassment, it was the one thing I left out of my later police statement because I was too mortified to tell anyone. It probably would have meant a longer prison sentence for Cooke had I had the courage to speak out sooner. This is still a very hard part of my story to share with anyone, but if I left it out I would be failing to demonstrate just how sick an individual Eamonn Cooke is.

The abuse didn't stop immediately after this incident but it did start to give me a clear idea that something wasn't right. There was still my unease at thinking my gran could see me in Cooke's bed, and then my fear over the question of where babies came from. Seeing him perform oral sex on a girl had shocked me, and now Cooke's acts were causing me both pain and fear, things I'd never experienced in those first years of abuse. Slowly, parts of the jigsaw puzzle were falling into place. A fuller picture was emerging and now I knew for certain that his behaviour wasn't right. But I was trapped and scared and didn't know what to do about it.

<u>6</u>

Some time around 1977, Cooke became more heavily involved in a pirate radio show called Radio Dublin. The station had started up in 1966 but he had first become interested in it in 1974 when the show's transmitter broke down and he was asked to fix it. He maintained an interest in Radio Dublin, which at the time only broadcast on Sunday afternoons. But by 1977 he realised that listeners wanted more than just a weekend alternative to RTE, the state broadcaster. At that point he gave up his television repair shop and went full-time into running Radio Dublin, recruiting a team of young and vibrant staff to help him. While he didn't launch the original radio station, he was certainly responsible for re-branding it and for its huge success when he took over the helm. It made its money primarily through advertising revenue, although much of that, I understand, was ploughed back into the station to finance its rapid growth. Almost overnight, Cooke set up the station in his living room and our secret place, as we saw it, was gone. For the first couple of years he had been the only adult in the house when he abused us, but now there were lots of people around all the time. He didn't stop abusing children, but the opportunities certainly became less frequent. Sometimes there could be as many as eight other adults there, and on busy days such as these no abuse took place.

From the beginning, the new radio staff were used to seeing us children around the place. We would run errands for them, getting them coffee and biscuits or fetching them cigarettes. It was a welcome distraction for us. They were not connected to Cooke's abuse of us in any way. On the contrary, when they suspected all was not right at the house, his staff were the ones to blow the whistle on him and quickly left to work at other radio stations.

The transmission of Radio Dublin from his living room turned Eamonn Cooke into a household name in Ireland. Despite its amateur origins, broadcast from a cramped room in his dingy house, it became a huge success across the country. It was similar to Radio Luxembourg, then the most famous pirate radio station. Radio Dublin became our very own home-grown version. It was massively popular with young people because it was more exciting than anything the public had encountered before. The national broadcaster then was RTE, which translates as Radio Television Ireland, our equivalent of the BBC. It seemed far more stuffy and old-fashioned than Radio Dublin.

Almost overnight Cooke was seen as a public hero and became known as the self-proclaimed 'granddaddy of Irish radio'. He earned the nickname of 'Captain Cooke' – or 'The Captain' for short. He even had his own 'Captain's address' when he went on air once a week to broadcast to his listeners.

He was rarely out of newspaper headlines because of the controversy surrounding his pirate station. A team of enthusiastic staff worked for him, and it was seen as cool and hip to get a job with 'The Captain'. For the first time, youth culture had its own public voice; Cooke always championed the underdog on his show. Despite its popularity, though, the station was illegal because it didn't have a licence to broadcast, so there were often police raids at the house to try and shut the station down. But after each one Cooke started back up again, which only seemed to increase his popularity. He organised protest marches through the streets of Dublin, lobbying for a licence so he could operate legally. Thousands of people turned out to support him. Cooke loved to stick two fingers up at authority and relished this fight with bureaucracy and its red tape that held the airwaves in a stranglehold.

But the people who idolised Captain Cooke had no idea about his dark side; the persona we still called the Cookie Monster. He was a man leading an incredible double life. They had no inkling that this much-respected and loved DJ was molesting and abusing young children in the very house from which their favourite radio station broadcast.

I remember when it all started. Inside the house it was suddenly chaotic. Cooke had rigged up all sorts of electrical instruments and installed some record decks. The DJs began broadcasting almost as soon as the equipment had been set up, and the middle room was taken over by people sitting at desks and answering the telephones when listeners rang in with their requests. The telephonists would say, 'Radio Dublin, can I take your request, please?'

That was the job I really wanted to do because I wanted to wear a badge that said 'Telephonist'. It seemed to be both important and fun. The staff were of mixed ages, but mainly they were in their late-teens and early-twenties.

Radio Dublin was the latest thing for the city and everyone wanted to be a part of it. I seemed to become the most popular girl in school overnight because all my classmates were talking about how Siobhan Kennedy worked at the pirate radio station! I was delighted when I was given the job of writing out the song and message requests on bits of paper to pass to the DJs. I got my name badge with the Radio Dublin logo on it and felt really cool.

The advent of Radio Dublin also meant an end to the secrecy about the children's presence in Cooke's house. Everyone in the community knew about the radio station, and my parents knew a lot of the local kids were popping in and out with requests and running errands for the staff. Because it was now seen as a place of work, this was okay with local parents. It was viewed as a very different thing from going into someone's private house. As some of his closest neighbours, my parents would now even pass pleasantries with Cooke, saying things such as, 'I bet those kids are driving you mad since you opened your radio? They never leave you alone.'

They simply had no idea about him.

Nobody took much notice of us kids, and certainly in the early days nobody had any suspicions of Cooke. The abuse had subsided but it hadn't stopped. He would still abuse us in the garage, taking great risks to do so when the DJs were on air. He even took me into his bedroom to abuse me while downstairs there were DJs broadcasting from his living room. I was just too young to understand the man's audacity and arrogance in preying on children when there were adults in the house, oblivious to his behaviour.

On quieter days, when there was just a receptionist downstairs taking phone calls, he would carry on his abuse as normal. By this stage, he allowed most of us kids to answer the telephones and take requests from the general public. I subsequently learned at his trial that he used this same tactic for years to lure more young children into his home.

The house became so busy with all the people involved in Radio Dublin that even his wife grew used to seeing us kids around. Later, at Cooke's trial, she confirmed she had seen us there and described how she used to give us bread and jam for snacks.

As the radio station's popularity grew, certain children visited the house less and less. Their parents felt they were spending too much time in the place, but remained in blissful ignorance that anything sinister was happening there.

Cooke was seen as the man who gave many young DJs their first start. A lot of broadcasters who are now very famous in Ireland started their careers at Radio Dublin, including Marty Whelan, Dave Fanning, John Clarke and James Dillon. I remember one of them drove a sporty little VW Beetle and I was very impressed by it. To me, it looked like something straight out of the Herbie films, which were very popular at the time.

Radio Dublin was funky compared to anything else on the airwaves and was above all a pop music station offering requests. One of my favourite songs at the time was 'Black is Black', which had a lot of air time.

Some people thought Radio Dublin the best thing ever, others didn't because it was illegal, but right or wrong it was *the* rebel station of the time, which propelled it into Irish broadcasting history.

I adored the radio station; couldn't wait to go down there and be at the heart of the buzz. However, by now I had decided that I definitely didn't like Cooke touching me. With the naivety of the child I was, I figured I could continue going to the radio station, but would just have to avoid Cooke. He, of course, had other ideas, and continued to abuse me whenever the opportunity arose.

Every time I hadn't been able to escape his groping hands, or worse, I would return home and, while I waited for Mammy to open the front door, would use a stone to scratch a mark on the brickwork of our house, as a reminder to myself not to return there. But somehow I always did. The marks I scored are still on our wall today, a painful reminder now of how little I could do to protect myself.

It didn't work because, by then, Cooke was getting more aggressive and threatening in his behaviour. I believe he also sensed that, as I was getting older, I was starting to withdraw from him. When he tried to put his hands on me, I began asking him to go away and leave me alone. I asked him not to touch me anymore. The first time that happened was after he had abused me in his bed. I kept thinking that if anyone could see me there, it wouldn't look good and people would think I wasn't a very nice girl. I also kept thinking of my gran looking down on me. I was a few months shy of my eleventh birthday and the crosses scored on the wall of my house were getting bigger and bigger.

Cooke would constantly tell me he could read my thoughts. He told me that brainwaves were the same as the airwaves which transmitted the songs on his radio station. I was terrified to hear that he knew what I was thinking. I clearly believed him, because when I went to the toilet, I used to wonder if he had it bugged or not. I couldn't understand how he knew what was in my mind, when in reality it was just another way he used to control me and keep me in fear of even thinking of telling anyone what he did to me.

I remember the first time he directly threatened me. He said that if I stopped going to his house, he would scatter nude photos of me all over the dashboard of his car so that my mammy and daddy would see them. I was in his car when he said this and he was angry with me because I had said that I didn't want to go back to his house. He threatened another girl with something very similar, saying he would scatter nude pictures of her all over the street.

He would always follow his threats by softening and saying: 'You're my special girl, come here to me.'

I don't remember ever posing for him to take my picture, but certainly he always had cameras around. To this day I have no idea if he secretly photographed or filmed me in his bedroom. In today's Internet age when so much pornographic material is shared online by perverts, this thought still haunts me. His other victims have since told me that Cooke threatened to put them in a home or have them taken away by the police if they told on him or refused to let him abuse them. Not surprisingly, they too were always called his 'special girl'. I suspect by this stage Cooke had begun to worry that any outspoken child would pose a threat to his double life.

As the debate about Radio Dublin rumbled on, Cooke continued to organise marches and demonstrations through the streets of the city, lobbying to be granted a legal licence to broadcast. The hierarchy of Catholic Ireland, of course, thought a pop music station sinful and wanted it stopped. On one occasion, the staff rigged out this huge float to drive through the streets, and I was desperate to be involved. At first Cooke said no, but eventually he relented and I begged Mammy to let me go. She organised for an older girl at the station to mind me for the day and believed, as always, that I was perfectly safe. She believed the people who were looking after me were trustworthy and responsible young adults. Ironically, I was far safer in the streets and under the public gaze than I ever was in the privacy of Cooke's house because he would not be rumbled for a very long time. He continued to abuse children for another thirty years before he was finally jailed for his crimes. For each of those decades, he wrecked the lives of a different generation of victims, without remorse.

The march was pretty amazing and I thought I was really cool and hip, singing and dancing as we sashayed through the streets. Thousands came out to cheer us on our way and show their support for the station. There was music blaring out and the day had a real carnival atmosphere. It also effectively distracted me from Cooke's continuing abuse, and I went back to believing he was a nice man for letting me take part in the demo, which was most likely his thinking behind letting me be involved in the first place.

Cooke spoke to me about some of the older girls who came to his house and said he paid them lots of money because they let him put his erection inside them. Over the years, I have seen some of these girls grow into young adults. They don't know me but I know them to be fellow victims of his vile abuse.

Cooke was still using money as an incentive too, and at the house we'd continue to compare the differing amounts he gave us. But I was growing increasingly unsettled by what he was doing and why exactly we were being given the money. I didn't want to do anything with him anymore, despite the money and the competitive atmosphere he had created. That was when I started to ask questions of the other girls.

I would say, 'Do you get into Mr Cooke's bed, and does he touch you?'

They all said yes, but oddly none of us was embarrassed to talk about it or voiced any feeling of awkwardness. One friend told me years later that after his abuse of her she spent her entire life feeling inadequate, as if she were always being compared to someone 'better' than her. She also felt extremely mistrustful about accepting money from any source, even legitimate employment. A lot of the attitudes he instilled in us as children, such as not feeling good enough, have been very hard to shake off in adulthood, leading to lifelong low self-esteem and depression in some of his victims. As youngsters we remained hyper-competitive with each other even after the abuse stopped, not realising that it was because of the damage Cooke had inflicted on us as vulnerable little people.

Looking back, it's extraordinary to think that he got away with so much. Significantly, if he'd ever tried to kiss us, we would instantly have known it was wrong, as a result of playing kiss chase with our mates. It would have automatically seemed grotesque and twisted to us as kids because we could make a comparison with the innocent games we played in our own peer group. We knew that kissing was something only grown-ups should do and so it was something for us kids to run away from.

His sexual abuse of us, however, was a standard of behaviour that had been set by him and we knew no different. Until we met him, it didn't even figure in our consciousness. At the age of ten I still did not associate his abuse with sex or with anything wrong – I just knew I didn't like it.

7

Cooke's free rein over my body finally came to an end in 1978 following a chance conversation I had with some of the female staff working for him at the radio station. They were girls I looked up to because they seemed so much more grown-up and sophisticated than me. I can't remember the precise details now, but I told them about the pornographic magazines and how Cooke had said I would have big boobies like the models when I grew up. I was laughing as I told them this and one of the girls asked: 'Why are you laughing – are you laughing at the diddies?'

'Ah, no,' I replied. 'I've seen loads of pictures of them upstairs in Mr Cooke's back room, hidden behind the tellies.'

She carried on chatting to me and asked me some more questions about the pictures. I was a bit frightened and remember being worried that Cooke would be listening in and would know I was betraying him.

'Don't say too much in here because Mr Cooke knows everything you think and say,' I warned her. Then she asked me if he had shown me the pictures of the naked ladies, and I told her that he had. I didn't know it at the time, but after she left me she went straight off to report this conversation.

A few days later, one of the other girls sought me out and asked if I would go to her house and make a tape recording of my voice for the radio. I was just delighted to be asked and didn't link it in any way to our earlier chat. Two of the girls took me off to make the recording.

They sat me down and set the tape-machine going and began to ask me lots of questions about Cooke. They asked if I went to the radio station a lot, and what I did in the house. They asked me if I had ever seen Mr Cooke with no clothes on, and I replied, 'Of course I have, all the time.' Then they questioned me about his anatomy and asked me to describe various parts of his body. I was getting a bit giggly and embarrassed by this point. Then, when they asked me to describe what was in Cooke's trousers, I fell about laughing. 'It looks like a banana,' I squealed between my hysterics. I don't recall all the other questions, but I was more than willing to answer whatever I could. I can't even remember how the girls reacted. I just thought it was all a big laugh and part of the show they were recording for the radio.

Within days, the fallout from my revelations began. One of my friends came running up to me in the street, roaring at me and crying uncontrollably.

'What's wrong?' I asked her.

'The girl from the radio station has told my sister that we've been in Cooke's house and he's touched our bums! My sister has called me a slut and said she's going to tell our mammy and daddy. And it's all *your* fault . . . you with your big mouth!'

My friend was furious with me and also scared that everything was going to come out about us being in Cooke's house. Even at this point, we believed only we were in the wrong. I just scampered off home, running my fingers over the scratches by the door as I waited for Mammy to let me in, and praying to God that our secret wouldn't come out.

I am not sure precisely when the abuse stopped but I do know that the last time I went to Cooke's house was in the spring of 1978. I was almost eleven years old. I had been worried after my friend shouted at me for making that tape but nothing happened at first. It must have been a week or two later when the bombshell I'd been dreading finally dropped on our family.

I was at home and saw one of the parish priests walking up the pathway to our front door. It was Father Jimmy Nolan and there seemed nothing unusual about this visit. I certainly didn't immediately suspect it had anything to do with the row I'd had with my friend or with what Cooke had been doing. I heard Mammy let him in – and then I froze with horror at what he said next.

'I have something I'd like to discuss with you, Mrs Kennedy, and I'd like to speak to you in private, if that's okay? Perhaps it might be best if the children went out to play?'

Well, I didn't know what was up, but instinctively I knew something was wrong. I went out but was scared stiff that I was in some kind of trouble. I went and found some of the friends who had been in Cooke's house with me.

'The priest is in my house and something's up,' I confessed. Everyone reacted with horror and I just knew I was going to be in a lot of bother when I went home.

Eventually Mammy called me in, and from the moment I walked through the door, I could see she didn't seem right; her face looked different, with an expression I'd never seen on it before.

It turned out that the girls from Radio Dublin who had recorded my conversation about Cooke had given the tape to James Dillon, the station manager. He had listened to it and became convinced that Cooke had sexually abused me. He decided that the best thing to do was to ask one of the local employees of the station to deliver the tape to our parish priest. It fell to Father Nolan to break the news to Mammy. I didn't learn the full details of his visit until many years later, when I was old enough to understand more, but this is how my mammy Kathleen remembers that dreadful moment.

'The day that Father Nolan broke the news to me about Siobhan was the day my heart broke. He asked me to sit down because he had something serious to discuss and my first thought was that one of the kids had done something terribly wrong. I didn't have a clue what he was about to tell me.

'He explained that a tape recording of Siobhan had found its way to the parish church and that it contained information that pointed to Eamonn Cooke sexually abusing my daughter. He didn't have the tape with him that day; in fact, I have never seen or heard the tape. I can't remember Father Nolan's exact words because from the moment I heard that Siobhan had been abused, I froze and went into some kind of shock. My head was ringing and some of his words sounded blurred. I could barely take in the details because I couldn't believe what I was hearing. I know I felt sick because I couldn't believe there were people who could do such things to children. I had never considered Siobhan, or any of my children, to be in any danger when they were out playing, especially not from a man who lived in our community. I kept muttering that it couldn't be true and I was shaking. I must have looked ashen because I felt all the blood drain from my head and my legs just went weak from the horror.

'My first reaction was to go to the police with this information, but when I asked the priest what I should do he advised me not to go to them. Instead he told me to take my daughter to the doctor and have her examined. He said a doctor would be able to tell if anything bad had happened to Siobhan. He also said it could be more damaging to her if I went to the police and the abuse was made public.

'Ireland in the 1970s still lived with a culture of secrecy and shame about sexual matters. If your priest told you to do something, you accepted it as the right course of action. The clergy were the pillars of our community, we all looked to them for advice on how to lead our lives, so I agreed to do what he said.

'Hearing the news of what had happened to Siobhan was the worst day of my life; it is every parent's worst nightmare. But what I couldn't get my head around then was how or why anyone would do this to a child. Parents were still very naive about paedophiles in those times, unlike today when families are much more informed and warned to be on their guard against perverts like Cooke. I had nowhere to turn, no website or phoneline to tell me how to deal with this situation. All I knew was that someone had hurt my firstborn baby and that made me sick to my stomach.'

Nothing was said to me until my daddy came home. Mammy must have told him what had gone on because they both sat me down then and said there were some things they needed to know. I was terrified I was in trouble, but they were very gentle with me. They said they wanted to know about what happened when I went down to Radio Dublin; they promised I wasn't in any trouble, but I was still scared. They started asking me questions about Cooke and his behaviour, and I remember it was then that Mammy just lost control. Whatever I had said to her had obviously confirmed his abuse of me and she started crying hysterically – she was devastated – and I was very frightened because I had never seen her like this before. Daddy tried to comfort her but nothing seemed to help.

When she was calm again, Mammy and Daddy told me not to worry, that everything would be okay. But it didn't feel that way to me because I had never seen Mammy cry so hard before. They explained that I would have to go and see a doctor. I just nodded in agreement. The following day Mammy took me down to see our local GP. She explained that I would have to have an examination, and that if I was a good girl I would get a packet of sweets afterwards. I still remember being rewarded with a bag of Jelly Tots.

The doctor asked me to lie down. I wasn't in the slightest bit embarrassed at being examined 'down there'. It was something I had become all too familiar with. I don't remember a vaginal examination, but I do recall a back passage examination because I didn't like it and it hurt. I then remember the doctor having a conversation with Mammy right in front of me. I don't know if he thought I wouldn't take in what he was saying, but I can still recall his words today.

He said he couldn't see any signs of penetration, which in his view was the worst thing that could have happened to me. He also said I seemed fine in myself and that as I was a very young child, I would probably forget what had happened. He then said there was a possibility I might have a few emotional repercussions in the years to come and that it was my mental stability Mammy would have to monitor in the future. I still had no concept of sexual activity, but remember no one thought to ask if Mr Cooke had put his fingers or his mouth anywhere on my body; the doctor's main concern was to establish if any penetrative sex had taken place. Mammy then told the doctor she was going to go to the police but he advised her not to because he felt it would inflict greater anguish on me if the abuse were ever to become public knowledge.

As we left his surgery that day I felt less scared, just happy to get my bag of sweets as a treat. But my parents were far from happy with the advice of the doctor and so Mammy decided to take me to see a second GP. I had to go through another examination and this time I remember it involving a vaginal examination. I got a box of Smarties this time. Mammy received the same advice: that all in all it was probably better for me if we keep the abuse secret and don't go to the police. She virtually collapsed in distress as we left the surgery. It wouldn't be until many years later that I realised the terrible hurt and grief she too had suffered because of Cooke's abuse of me.

A short while later, I came home from playing to find Sylvia, one of the female DJs from the station, sitting in the living room with my mammy and one of my aunties. Sylvia was one of the top female DJs in Ireland at the time. She revealed that Cooke had been on holiday in Spain but when he returned he discovered his radio station had been virtually destroyed by some of the staff in his absence.

Mammy asked me to go to my room then but instead I sat on the stairs outside so I could listen to what they were saying. I heard Mammy asking Sylvia if she realised what kind of a man Cooke was. Mammy knew she had children of her own. Sylvia was a lovely woman and would have had no idea that Cooke was such a monster. I was holding my favourite doll as I listened to their conversation; she was a beautiful Chinese doll with lots of black hair tied up in a bun, but by the end of Sylvia's visit I had pulled all the hair out of her head without even realising I was doing it. I loved that doll but I destroyed her that day through my fear of something I didn't totally understand.

Cooke got away with so much back then because of the era we lived in; it was a far cry from the days of vigilante mobs throwing bricks at paedophiles' houses. Ordinary people then didn't have the confidence or the knowledge that they do today. Many things were swept under the carpet through sheer ignorance or embarrassment, and it wasn't until much later on, when the lid was blown off the sex abuse that had been so rife within parts of the Catholic Church itself, that ordinary people began to understand how villains like Cooke had got away with their crimes for so long. People didn't speak about deviants like Cooke then; in fact, they didn't speak about sex at all. Mammy and Daddy knew I had been 'interfered with', but they had no idea how to deal with the fact. It just wasn't something they could express or act upon within the limits of their world. For now, Cooke had won because there was no one who would listen to us and help us through this trauma.

In a very different way, Mammy and Daddy were also innocent victims of Cooke. I knew Mammy just couldn't get her head around the fact this had really happened; she didn't disbelieve it, but she had never before imagined such things went on. My parents didn't sweep Cooke's abuse of me under the carpet through fear. They simply followed the advice of the most respected members of their society, the clergy and the doctors. These people had not committed any abuse against me themselves but, as far as I'm concerned, they were complicit in it. Their silence enabled Cooke to remain undetected by the law for decades, and granted him the freedom to abuse generations of children.

Mammy remembers one very poignant example of the religious mores of the times we lived in, one I am sure many other Catholic women of the same era will recall. It says a lot about the naivety and innocence of ordinary families with regard to the preaching of the Catholic Church, but back then our religion dictated that sex was purely a function of the procreation of life; our Church decreed it was not something you should actually enjoy or take pleasure from. When a woman gave birth to a child, therefore, she was expected to go to her priest and receive a special blessing known as 'churching'. It was intended to cleanse her in case she had enjoyed the sexual act that led to the conception of her newborn. That was the hard line of the Catholic Church. I have this vision of women all over Ireland going before their priests to be blessed in case they had enjoyed sex with their husbands . . . something that young people in today's society would never be able to understand. Having a baby with your husband is the most natural and loving thing in the world, but by ordering women to be 'cleansed' afterwards the Church was stigmatising sex even within marriage as dirty and sinful. If that was how Mammy was forced to feel about having her own children, then how on earth was she supposed to cope with the worse horror of knowing a grown man had sexually abused one of them?

The revelation of Cooke's abuse of me caused huge ructions and panic among some of my friends in the neighbourhood. I learned that James Dillon had led a mini-rebellion against Cooke after listening to the tape. Certain that Cooke had abused me, he called a staff meeting to inform the others of his fears. He said he was leaving Radio Dublin and invited them to join him in starting up a new station.

Similarly, I called a meeting of a group of my pals at the telegraph pole round the back of my house. These were the friends who had been in Cooke's house with me and we all huddled around conspiratorially as I delivered the bad news to them.

'Okay, okay,' I declared dramatically. 'People now know we used to go into Cooke's house and what he used to do. My mammy is after bringing me to the doctor's, and Cooke definitely shouldn't have been doing what he did to us because that's your privates "down there" and no one is supposed to touch them.'

As I started telling them this, one by one they all started roaring, crying and screaming.

'What's wrong?' I questioned.

'Our mammies are going to be called now, and we're all going to be in big trouble,' one of the girls piped up.

So we decided that the best thing for us to do was run away to Memorial Park, near our homes. We were going to build our own dens there and hide so that no one could find us. That was our master plan, anyway, but everything depended on what my mammy was going to do. Everyone was sweating in their beds for a couple of nights, waiting to see if Mrs Kennedy was going to tell all the other mammies.

Mammy had instinctively wanted to go to other parents in the neighbourhood so that they could speak to their children and find out if Cooke had harmed them too. The doctors and the clergy, however, had advised her differently. All three professionals that Mammy spoke to recommended she didn't approach other families in case her own child then bore the backlash for Cooke's crimes. In other words, they thought that other parents might, in some way, assume I was to blame for anything that had happened to their children. It sounds like something from a distant century, I know, but that was the way of thinking then.

Mammy was tortured by this advice because she felt she should warn others that their children were at risk, but her first priority was her own daughter. If there was even the slightest chance I could be further hurt she wasn't prepared to take it, and so she heeded the professional advice that was given to her. As it turned out, Mammy was in some ways right to keep quiet because very soon I started to be shunned by some of the families in our community.

For the other kids who had been in Cooke's house, it was a huge relief that Mrs Kennedy didn't tell their parents. It meant we didn't all have to run away, and life resumed as normal. At least, it did for most of them. For me it was different. Gradually, gossip spread and I became known as the child Cooke had abused. Mammy never made my ordeal at his hands public knowledge; the only ones who knew the full facts were her closest relatives, and they were a great support to her at the time. It was inevitable, though, that word leaked out. It was a small, tight-knit community, and rumours and innuendo were soon flying about like wildfire. People knew something was amiss just from the fact that James Dillon and some of the staff had walked out. Despite Mammy's best efforts to protect me, I started to feel the backlash of people's response to the gossip. There is no doubt I was cast as the chief villain in a few households locally.

I will never forget the day that one of my friends came up to me in the street and said she was no longer allowed to play with me. I was devastated and remember feeling totally worthless. Ironically, the feeling that Cooke had bred within me was reinforced by people who didn't know any better than to blame the victim of his abuse. I was desperately upset and went home crying. If it wasn't bad enough that he had abused me, now my friends were being warned to stay away from me. Mammy told me not to worry, but she was distraught for her child. There was nothing she could do to stop this backlash that the priest and the doctors had warned her about. She hid her despair very well, though; it was only in later years that I learned the extent of her suffering.

The following day the same thing happened again. A second girl came up and said her mammy had said she had to stay away and that she wasn't allowed to play with me anymore. It seemed that some parents had heard about Cooke and what he'd done to me in his house, and didn't want their children to be tarred with the same brush. It was a typical enough reaction for that time – completely failing to take into account the real villain of this story.

The reaction in the neighbourhood reinforced Mammy's decision not to speak to other parents. She could see that I was being demonised for something that had been done to me, suggesting I myself had done wrong. I believe that in fact some families locally were terrified of facing up to what that man had done to me, and what potentially he might have done to their own children. Others simply didn't believe that the same thing could possibly have happened to their child. To them I was nothing but a bad influence that their kids had to stay away from. Fortunately, not all the kids shunned me, which was a great relief. But while I went to school as normal and we continued to go out as a family, so far as playing out was concerned, I was never allowed out of Mammy's sight from that day on.

I thought it very unfair that some people thought it was all my fault, and as hard as Mammy tried to console me, I still ended up feeling as if I *had* done something wrong. I suppose in a way it was a bit like when someone dies. Some people would rather cross the street than face bereaved relatives, because they don't know what to say. The Catholic community of Inchicore did not know how to deal with my situation. I understand that now, but at the time it was devastating. My parents had to try and live with what their neighbour had done to me in a way that caused the least amount of suffering to their daughter; I can only imagine what horrors they must have been through as parents of a victim of child abuse.

Emotionally, there was no immediate fall out for me because I still didn't understand the severity of Cooke's crimes against me. Years later, when the impact of his abuse finally hit me, I would realise how deep it had cut into me; how it had left me feeling like damaged goods.

I know now that Cooke affected many lives in our community; abused many children, some of whom I never knew. After I later gave evidence against him in court, many women came up to me and confided that they had been in Cooke's house and that he had abused them too. I hadn't even known some of them back in my childhood, when we were all just innocent young girls. It just goes to show how wide-ranging and prolonged his evil influence was.

8

Despite the local gossip and increasing awareness that Cooke had abused a child, for the time being it appeared that he had slipped through the net. Remarkably, he even continued to live in the same house and no one confronted him about his actions. In a society where consensual adult sex outside of marriage was seen as sinful, and even someone who had sex within marriage had to be 'cleansed', many people were simply too frightened to face up to what this depraved individual in their midst had done to an innocent child.

Cooke needed to abuse children like he needed oxygen to breathe, but the one other thing he loved most in life was his radio station. It was an integral part of his world and remained so until he was jailed nearly thirty years later. It would also feature heavily during his trials. Cooke tried to use the station and its staff as a defence against the accusations about his child sex abuse. He always, falsely, maintained that I was forced to make up allegations against him to blacken his name so that rival disc jockeys, led by James Dillon, could close him down and emulate his success with their own station.

Indeed, he tried to convince two juries that when all his staff walked out after hearing allegations of abuse against him, it was merely a business tactic. Cooke actually believed he was untouchable. He was so supremely arrogant that when the scandal first broke in 1978 he even went to the media to report on the so-called 'conspiracy' against himself and Radio Dublin. Headlines in national papers screamed 'Mutiny on the Airwaves', and Cooke successfully diverted the press's attention away from the real reason his station had been trashed.

The following article, which was accompanied by a picture of Cooke at his record decks, appeared in the *Irish Press* on Monday 10 April 1978, under the headline of 'Staff "Mutiny" in Radio Dublin':

> Staff at Radio Dublin have 'mutinied'. On his return from a Spanish holiday, Captain Eamonn Cooke, head of the station, said he found that broadcasts had stopped and almost all the twenty-strong staff had gone – apparently to start a new airwave pirate called The Big D. He said last night that allegations had been made about his personal conduct during his absence. 'Nobody even approached me about these allegations but it appears that the staff have left as a result of them.' Mr Cooke said he strongly denied the allegations. 'It appears that seven days' absence on holiday was too long. Perhaps I made a mistake and should never have gone,' he said.

*

When rumours of child abuse surfaced in broadcasting trade publications, Cooke took the radical step of bringing the accusations into the open himself. He knew about the tape and he knew that James Dillon was certain he had abused me. The following Sunday 16 April 1978, Cooke went on air on Radio Dublin to make a two-hour news broadcast about the 'mutiny' and to defend himself against the allegations. He openly denied any wrongdoing. In doing so, he gambled that the public would believe this proved he had nothing to hide. Cooke had a lot of supporters throughout the radio community and, for the time being, it was a gamble that paid off. He thrived on all the attention and publicity, and loudly maintained he was an innocent man who had been framed by duplicitous rivals seeking to hijack his success.

His message to the public was bold and clear. He was saying, *If I have done something wrong, then why have I not been arrested or even questioned by the Garda? These are all just nasty slurs and rumours designed to blacken my name, but I have nothing to hide.*

He then played his ace by recruiting Father Michael Cleary to work for him on Radio Dublin. Cleary was quite simply a legend throughout Ireland, idolised by the entire nation. He was known as 'The Singing Priest' because he would travel the country staging cabaret performances in front of thousands, to raise cash for needy causes. He was also a TV celebrity, a newspaper columnist, and a friend to the very rich and powerful throughout Ireland. Cooke was about to add to that list of occupations by making him a radio star too.

Cleary was always the life and soul of any gathering and would effortlessly take to a stage and crack jokes or sing songs. He was larger than life, tall and gangly, with wisps of dark hair and a huge bushy beard. He formed part of the clergy working at the parish of Ballyfermot, a sprawling, working-class district neighbouring Inchicore. A small bridge was all that separated the two areas and local parishioners often worshipped in churches to either side of the geographical border. Cleary was not just famous in our neighbourhood but all over Ireland for his musical work. God-fearing Catholics thought he was the next best thing to the Lord Almighty himself!

But he was also a man with a dark secret, for while publicly he was regarded as a living saint for all his charity work, behind presbytery doors he was secretly 'married' to a young girl called Phyllis Hamilton who had given birth to his two children. Publicly, people believed Phyllis was nothing more than his devoted housekeeper, but for three decades they lived together as man and wife.

Cleary's secret was not revealed until after he died. In 1995 Phyllis wrote her autobiography with the help of the brilliant crime reporter and author Paul Williams, who works for the *Sunday World*. Her revelations in the book *Secret Love* rocked the Catholic Church to its foundations, even though Phyllis clearly viewed her relationship with Cleary as a tragic love story. Ireland's favourite son, it turned out, had duped everyone by seducing a young girl when she was just seventeen.

Phyllis was clearly a troubled and vulnerable teenager when she approached Cleary and unburdened her soul to him in a confessional. From a broken home, she'd spent most of her childhood in orphanages or psychiatric homes. In her book she revealed how she fell in love with the charismatic priest who famously hosted a Mass for Pope John Paul II on his historic visit to Ireland. She also revealed how he was prone to dark rages and outbursts of cruelty towards her. Phyllis gave birth to Cleary's two sons, the first of whom was put up for adoption. She remained his secret lover for twenty-seven years, until his death. Phyllis herself has subsequently died.

In 1978, however, the unsuspecting Irish public had no idea about Cleary's double-life. By employing him on Radio Dublin, Cooke played a blinder, for when allegations of child abuse surfaced against 'The Captain', Cooke asked Cleary to go on air to defend him. The popular cleric made a public broadcast to say that his friend and colleague was a good man who was entirely innocent of the accusations made against him. He went on to say that the rumours were completely unfounded, and that Cooke had been the victim of a smear campaign designed to ruin him.

At that time, Cooke couldn't have been given a better reference if God Himself had dropped into the studio to defend him because Cleary's word was Gospel. If he said that Eamonn Cooke was an upright man, then that was that; Eamonn Cooke must be an upright man. In public, Cleary took the high moral ground on sex and religion – when in private he was sharing his bed with a pretty, young and vulnerable blonde. His devoted parishioners learned nothing of how he secretly trampled all over their unconditional trust of him for almost three decades.

Cleary was certainly guilty of rank hypocrisy and deceit but his secret love with Phyllis Hamilton was not the only scandal that would rock the parish of Ballyfermot. He would later be accused of a deed far more sinister than having sex with a vulnerable teenage girl. Disturbingly, it is also alleged that he covered up the paedophile abuses of a fellow priest in his parish.

In 2007, a child abuse support group in Dublin called One in Four highlighted on their website the following damning article about Cleary's role in covering up those crimes. This is how writer Mary Raftery revealed the true lyrics behind 'The Singing Priest':

> There is an element of rewriting history in the recent focus on the life and times of Father Michael Cleary. While people mull over whether he was a lying hypocrite or merely a sad victim of the Catholic Church's hard line on priestly celibacy, there is a crucially important part of his legacy that has been forgotten. Michael Cleary was guilty of covering up the most heinous of criminal activity. In the late 1970s and early 1980s, Cleary was senior curate in Ballyfermot. It was a position of some authority – Ballyfermot was at the time the largest parish in Dublin, with some five or six priests and a veritable army of upwards of sixty altar boys.
>
> One of the priests there at that stage was Tony Walsh, recently ordained and full of energy. Walsh was put in charge of the altar boys and ran the very popular Children's Mass. He joined the All Priests' Show and was, like Cleary, a well-known entertainer. He was also a serial child rapist, one of

the most vicious known paedophiles in the history of the Archdiocese of Dublin. His savage assaults on children spanned at least two decades, until he was finally caught and imprisoned in the mid-1990s. From 1979, Michael Cleary knew that Walsh was a paedophile.

Earlier that year, Walsh had targeted thirteen-year-old Ken Reilly, repeatedly sexually abusing him in the Ballyfermot parochial house. Ken eventually told his mother, Ena, what was happening, and she in turn reported it first to her own parish priest in Coolock before it came to Michael Cleary's attention in Ballyfermot.

Ena Reilly's description of her meeting with Cleary is instructive. She was at her wit's end with young Ken, who was becoming seriously emotionally disturbed. She wanted two things from Cleary: some help with Ken, and an assurance that Walsh would not abuse another child.

'He gave me a kind of lecture,' says Ena. 'He asked me had Ken been told the facts of life, and I said I thought he had. And he said he could have been aroused or something. But then he went on to tell funny jokes that people had come to him with, he turned it into a kind of a funny mood . . . silly old talk, and I came away disillusioned with the whole thing.'

Cleary, however, had a great reputation for the work he was doing with adolescents, and Ena did ask him to have a word with Ken himself. Ken was bemused by the whirlwind who arrived in the house one afternoon. 'He talked to me about the facts of life,' Ken remembers, 'about intimate touching between men and women, about how Tony Walsh was sorry for what he had done and was confused. They were the words that he used. And when he was leaving, he turned to my mother and said, "I'm after talking to Ken there. I'm after telling him about the facts of life." And then he marched out the door. And I was inside going, What the hell was he talking about? It was just absolute rubbish.'

Aside from the bizarre nature of this encounter, Cleary had, perhaps unwittingly, clarified a few matters for the Reillys. Firstly, it was evident that no one doubted the veracity of Ken's account of Walsh's abuse of him, and that Walsh appeared to have admitted his crime.

Secondly, it was apparent that as far as Cleary and Ballyfermot were concerned, the matter was now concluded. Walsh remained a priest in Ballyfermot for a further seven years. He had unlimited access to the parish children, being constantly in and out of the local primary schools. He abused well over a dozen children, including the particularly horrific and violent rape of a nine-year-old boy in the Phoenix Park.

When Walsh was finally moved in 1986, he was merely shifted to another parish, Westland Row, where he found new child victims. He left a wake of horror, misery and suicide behind him, much of which might have been prevented had Michael Cleary acted in 1979 on his certain knowledge that his fellow singing priest was a child abuser.

Cleary was certainly by no means alone in failing to protect children from the depredations of clerical paedophiles. But he did have one unique advantage – he was the people's darling, had an enormous media profile, and had just shot to international fame earlier in 1979 through his famous master of ceremonies role during Pope John Paul II's Youth Mass in Galway. A word from him, even the threat of publicity, could have made a profound difference to the way in which church authorities were busy covering up for child-abusing priests, and humiliating victims by refusing to take them seriously. No assessment of Michael Cleary can be complete without the inclusion of his silence in the face of such evil.

This report was a damning indictment of both Walsh and Cleary. Father Tony Walsh, one of Ireland's worst paedophile priests, was eventually defrocked and jailed for his crimes. After they were revealed, a report claimed that nearly every person in Ballyfermot knew of a friend, a brother or a cousin who had been abused by Walsh at some stage, such was the scale of his crimes.

Like Cleary, he was a popular entertainer in the 70s, and the two men would go on tour together and stage cabaret concerts. Walsh became known for his hip-grinding Elvis Presley imitations in their travelling priest talent show. He also knew Eamonn Cooke, and I somehow find it impossible to believe that two child abusers became friends by accident.

Cleary's involvement with two vicious child sex offenders suggests, at the very least, a serious lack of judgment when choosing his friends. I still have many unanswered questions about Cleary and his association with Cooke, in particular regarding the tape recording of me made by the staff of Radio Dublin.

During his first criminal trial in 2002, Cooke told the court that he was in possession of that tape of me talking about his abuse. It was the first I knew he had even heard it and one further public humiliation, knowing that he had been able to listen to my childish account of his abuse of me. He refused to say who gave him the tape but I have never been in any doubt that Father Michael Cleary was in some way instrumental in getting it to him. The priests in the neighbouring parishes of Ballyfermot and Inchicore all knew each other well and Cleary was the most respected of them all. It would merely have been a matter of his asking and the tape would have been his. He was Cooke's friend and publicly refuted the allegations against him. Now that Cleary's dead I will never find out just how much he knew about Cooke, but history has shown that he did cover up the horrific sexual crimes of another colleague, and I find it hard to believe he'd have behaved any differently for Cooke.

Mammy has never seen or heard the tape that was made that day and Father Jimmy Nolan did not have it with him the day he visited her. As far as I know, Father Jimmy was one of the good guys; he had a reputation for being a kind and gentle man. Sadly, he died while still a comparatively young man in 1988. He was sent to America for medical treatment because it was claimed he was an alcoholic and was found dead in the grounds of the clinic he was attending. He was in his forties, another sad case of a washed-up priest bearing who knows what heavy secrets of the Catholic Church.

In the 1990s many more paedophile priests would come to light and the Catholic Church in Ireland would face its biggest ever crisis. Not only did many priests harm small children, but senior Church figures knew about their crimes and covered them up. Instead of exposing their sickness to the world, they simply moved offenders around the country when new cases of abuse came to light, which allowed them to continue assaulting children, unchecked, for twenty years. Shielding these paedophiles caused untold misery and torture for so many child victims. It was the ultimate betrayal, and one from which the standing of the Irish Catholic Church has never recovered.

I vehemently believe that in choosing to remain silent about Cooke's abuse, the Church shares some of the guilt for his crimes. Father Nolan was just the messenger that day, but his advice for us to keep quiet was quite unequivocal. Perhaps the Church feared that Cleary's known connection to Cooke might have damaged its own reputation. Who can say? Even if my family had gone public at the time, it would probably have made no difference. Who, after all, was going to believe an Inchicore housewife and a ten-year-old kid against the word of Ireland's much-revered Singing Priest?

9

I can only recall those early days of Cooke and Radio Dublin through the eyes of a child, but I am fortunate enough to have an advocate whose adult memories help to paint a fuller picture. James Dillon is an integral part of the story; the hero of it, you could say. Quite simply, Mammy believes he saved my life by risking his own security and reputation to stop Cooke from abusing me. He never doubted I was telling the truth and went on to give evidence against his former boss in both of his criminal trials, helping to secure his eventual conviction. After Cooke was jailed, I had my first adult meeting with James. It was an extremely emotional reunion in which I was finally able to thank him for his unswerving belief in and support of me.

He remembers those dark days with stark clarity. This is his account of them.

> When I first joined Radio Dublin in 1977, it was still operating only at weekends; it was very low transmission and so its impact on Dublin was not very significant in the early days. My initial

involvement was to bring in advertising to the radio station, the money from which Cooke used to buy a decent transmitter. It was just a part-time job for me, a couple of hours on Saturdays and Sundays, as I was also disc jockeying in nightclubs during the evenings. Before long, the improved transmitter brought in more listeners and Radio Dublin began broadcasting seven days a week. We began to get calls from shops and factories and a lot of people clearly liked what they were hearing. It went from this tiny little pirate show to a huge station in the space of about four to five weeks – it was quite amazing.

Cooke himself was a very distinctive character and very different from everyone else on the station. He was older than everyone else and even though he was only in his late-thirties, he seemed more like a man in his sixties. He was very thin and he frequently wore a suit, yet he was slightly dirty and never smart-looking. He was always smoking and would lean back in his chair and the ash would drop all over his suit. I remember this because I didn't smoke and thought it was quite disgusting. He didn't laugh much; he would smirk mainly, rather than join in any fun with the staff.

I was twenty-six at the time and was probably the oldest of all the DJ staff. Everyone wanted to get on air and be disc jockeys – I had been a DJ for five years by this time so I had some experience. Cooke's wife Joan wasn't there all the time. From time to time she would go missing from the house for long periods and Cooke maintained she was in hospital.

The radio station was a full-time job for Cooke but what struck me was, he appeared to have no real interest in making a lot of money from it, at least in those early days. As a young man, I was keen to make money and he allowed me to keep half of the advertising revenue I generated, which I felt was very generous. He used the remaining money to pay for transmitters and other electrical equipment needed to improve Radio Dublin. Things may have changed later on, but initially he certainly didn't seem to be driven by money. Instead, he seemed to get a buzz from sticking two fingers up to authority and by being the 'king-pin' of radio, so there was definitely an egotistical element to it.

There were always lots of people around at the station, but Cooke remained a loner; he didn't have real friends, just associates, who worked for him. He appeared to listen to his employees' opinions, but despite being fanatical about the station, he seemed less bothered about the DJs who were employed. Neither did he hold strong opinions about how the radio should be run or what records should be played. Being the boss was the most important thing to him.

Cooke was a softly spoken man but at times he could have a menacing tone about him. If a rival pirate station went off the air for some reason, he would imply that he was behind it without making any specific admissions. I always wondered just how far he was prepared to go.

His house was small, dirty and cluttered. The only station legally on air at the time was RTE, the official Irish channel, like the BBC, and they only had pop music for about two hours a week. This meant that people in factories and shops couldn't listen to pop records at work so there was a niche in the market for stations like Radio Dublin, which is why they took off so quickly. Requests also formed a big part of the station's format.

I remember from the start that there were always children around in the house, knoçking on the door with requests or helping out by going to the shops for the staff. It was impossible to keep track of them, though, as they seemed to come and go as they pleased so you never knew who was or wasn't there. Having the kids around didn't strike me as odd at first, because the station was completely unstructured and in the middle of a residential area. They found the radio station as exciting as everyone else. I did find it strange when, occasionally, Cooke would come downstairs with a face like a big red tomato. His excuse was that he had been too close to the transmitter. I didn't believe his explanation, but I didn't in a million years latch on to the idea he was red-faced because he had been upstairs abusing children.

Like many people, I just didn't consider that child abuse was taking place and I believe many of the parents felt it was a safe place for the kids because there were so many people around. While other radio stations sprang up around the country, Radio Dublin became massive and its name was synonymous with the new wave of pirate radio. We even had politicians coming on to the show, lobbying for it to be legalised. No matter how many times the authorities tried to close it down, it would always restart again and the sensible politicians recognised that there was no going back for the State. Pirate radio became a political issue in 1978, which Cooke loved. He also basked in his rebel status, and the truth was the government didn't really know what to do. Simply closing down a station day after day no longer became a viable option. When Radio Dublin was raided, it only served to draw in more listeners and even brought thousands of people on to the streets to protest.

There was a lot of folklore surrounding Cooke and some of it was less than savoury. When it came to technical expertise, Cooke really knew his stuff. There was one particular story about how he blew up a statue in a cemetery. I don't know if the story was true or false – I believe it to be true – but what was important about it was that it made him a scary person to take on. It sent out the message that he was prepared to resort to violence if he didn't like something.

It became obvious to the authorities they were not going to be able to shut the radio station down. This was good news for me, because I was already doing well in my nightclub work and now business was flourishing with Radio Dublin, which was a roaring success. Some weeks, my share of the advertising revenue was about £500, which was a huge amount of money for a young man in those days. It would not have made sense for me to try and sabotage something that was working so well in my interests, as Cooke would later try and claim in his trial. I wasn't being paid to be on air, but to bring in advertising and as I had always had an entrepreneurial flair, I saw this as a golden opportunity.

Things were going very well for everyone, but then in the spring of 1978 I first heard allegations of child sex abuse by Eamonn Cooke. I had heard suspicions from an acquaintance that Cooke had interfered with one of the young girls at the station and I was shocked. Then it was brought to my attention that Siobhan was said to have innocently revealed Cooke's behaviour to a girl who worked at the radio. I wasn't sure what to believe, but from the moment I heard the allegations, I knew things were never going to be the same again; either some poor bloke was going to have his good name ruined or, even worse, the rumours would turn out to be true. If this was the case, I felt the onus was on me to put a stop to it.

I wasn't quite sure what to do but decided to see if this girl would go back to Siobhan and talk to her again, but to be careful not to put words into her mouth. I also suggested she tape the conversation, so I could hear it back to try and establish if there was any substance to the rumours. It was the only way I could think of settling the matter once and for all. I certainly didn't think it was appropriate for me to approach Siobhan.

The girl and her friend, who also worked at Radio Dublin, went to see Siobhan together and made the tape recording. It was later delivered back to me and I listened to it in the privacy of my own home. I remember thinking the girls had done very well in the way they spoke to Siobhan, considering they were only teenagers themselves. I heard Siobhan tell them that Cooke had a banana in his trousers. She repeated Cooke's threats to her. He had told her, 'I have a picture of you in my bedroom and you know your mammy wouldn't like it if she knew you were here with me in the bedroom. If you don't keep coming back here, I will put the picture in the dash of my car and when your mammy is walking past, she will see it and she will be really angry with you. She will know you have told her lies.'

Once I heard these words I was absolutely convinced that Cooke had abused Siobhan. It struck me that none of the girls could have made such a thing up because it was such blatant, adult manipulation of a child. But it never occurred to me back then that there could be other children who had been harmed by him.

My initial response was: 'You bastard.' But I also knew I had to get him stopped, so rushing in without thinking was not a good option because Cooke is a clever and devious man. I instinctively knew he would deny any wrongdoing and try to talk his way out of the trouble he was in.

I didn't discuss anything with the other DJs because I was worried that if I confided in the staff word might get back to Cooke. As luck would have it, a local travel agency was giving the radio station a free holiday as a prize for us to give away and I thought the best idea was to make sure Cooke went too. This gave me the opportunity to call a meeting with the staff, in his absence, so he didn't have a chance to intimidate individuals. I knew from his reputation that he was capable of threatening people who worked against him. This was the first step in my plan, but I had to continue going in and out of the radio station, without saying a word, until he went away. This was very hard, given the way I felt towards him, but I didn't want him to know anything was going on.

Cooke eventually flew to Spain with the prize winner and some other radio personnel. The day after they left, I called an urgent meeting of all the staff. Between the DJs, technicians and sales workers, there were about thirty-five people there. Among them were several men who have become very well known in the Irish radio industry, including John Clarke, Dave Fanning and Marty Whelan. I considered whether to play the tape recording of Siobhan but decided against it, believing it was too personal. I thought it was sufficient for me to explain how I had heard the recording and that it was enough to convince me that the children going in and out of Cooke's house were at risk from him. This was the first time I had considered the implications of Cooke's abuse, not only for Siobhan but for the other children who visited the house also. Some of the guys who lived locally said that rumours had been going around for ages about Cooke, but obviously no one had taken them seriously. Those who heard the accusations for the first time were shocked.

I told the meeting I had decided to withdraw from Radio Dublin and set up an alternative station. I added that I would welcome anybody who wanted to join me. Everyone who was in that room that day left with me, but some would end up returning to work for Cooke later on. I believed then that everyone was leaving on a matter of principle because of the child abuse, but I was disappointed years later to discover that was not necessarily the case. I was shocked when some returned to Cooke.

I knew it would be a big shock for Cooke to

return from holiday to discover everyone had left his station. I hoped it would be enough to set off alarm bells within the community around him and that people would realise why we did it. However, what happened next was like mob rule. I thought it was important to leave the station intact, as Cooke had left it, but others thought differently. There were calls from some of the staff to burn the place to the ground and it was all getting a bit out of hand. I called for calm and reason, and things appeared to settle down. When I returned the next day, however, the house had been searched. I hadn't organised the search because I believed that if anyone did carry out a search, it should be the police. The transmitter had also been damaged, putting Radio Dublin off the air. I called in the technicians to try and fix the equipment and get the station working again. It turned out that a number of photographs of children had been found. Girls were photographed in their slips and knickers and boys were seen in their vests and underpants. I knew this was highly suspect. I didn't have the photographs and I believe a member of staff was asked to take them to the local parish priest, a normal course of events for the day. Communities still trusted the clergy to do the right thing.

The tape of Siobhan was never made to try and discredit Cooke to the other DJs, as he tried to claim many years later. If that were the case, I would have played the tape to the staff. Instead I decided to spare them the gory details and simply told them I had reason to believe Cooke was a danger to children. I also asked a member of staff who lived in the area to take the tape of Siobhan to the local parish priests, trusting they would take the most appropriate course of action, not least in counselling a local family.

By the time Cooke was due to return from his holiday, his house had been ransacked by some of the unrulier members of staff. I wasn't there when it happened and it was not something I had ordered or that I agreed with, but it was part of the mob mentality that had taken over when they discovered the true nature of the man they were working for. It had never been a tidy place, but it was definitely ransacked; records were strewn over the room, doors ripped from their hinges, drawers were tipped out – it was a real mess. Those who were involved claimed they had been looking for more evidence against Cooke.

We launched an alternative station called The Big D in Dublin and went on air before Cooke got back from Spain. The plan had been to hand him back the keys to an empty radio station, but it had got a lot messier than that. On the day Cooke returned, I felt it was my responsibility to explain to him what had gone on and why people had left. A colleague and I went to Dublin Airport to meet him and I confronted him there and then.

I looked him in the eyes and said, 'Eamonn, accusations have been made against you that you have been abusing a child. I, for one, believe they are true.'

He cut me short, saying, 'Is the radio station still on the air?'

'No,' I replied.

With that he stormed off in a rage. I had accused him of child abuse, which should have been a huge body blow, but his only concern was for the radio station. As he continued to walk through the airport, I added, 'Eamonn, you have brought all this on yourself.' He was clearly furious but didn't threaten me or ask any questions about the accusations.

The following day, he got the radio station back on air. He then invited the *Sunday World* newspaper into his home to take photos of the mess in his house and gave a story to them about what he described as the sabotage of his radio station. He even had the nerve to say to the newspaper that staff had gone so far in their conspiracy as to make up stories about child abuse. He was the one who brought it out into the open, painting himself as the victim. The newspaper asked some of the staff why we had left the station and we just said that we could no longer work with Eamonn Cooke.

Cooke no longer had any DJs so he spent a lot of time on the air himself, moaning and complaining about those he blamed for trashing his station. It had the desired impact in Inchicore at least, because some people still supported him. When we arrived a week later to do a regular disco at a social event in the area, we were told we were not wanted there anymore. Some local people seemed almost to feel hatred towards Cooke's former staff. Ironically, those who were trying to help the community ended up being vilified by it. We received hate mail and protests for what was seen as our act of wanton destruction and malice. They had no idea of the real motive behind our actions. Cooke went on to speak publicly to other newspapers about how he went away on holiday and came back to find his radio station wrecked. He claimed we had operated out of greed and a perceived opportunity to go and do our own thing. He had no fear of repercussions and I believe he thought he was untouchable. He used the accusations against him as a tactic to try and prove he was being set up.

He then started a programme of intimidation against some of his former staff. He began following people in his car, and some were genuinely scared. I decided I would go up and see him at the radio station. When I arrived, he had a new group of cronies around him, men with walkie-talkies outside the house, pacing up and down. He had created a siege mentality. Three of them walked in with me and brought me to Eamonn who was sitting down. It was like Inchicore's answer to *The Godfather*.

'Eamonn, this intimidation has to stop,' I said to him.

'James, you have been lied to and you have been manipulated,' he replied. 'The reason you were chosen is because they all knew you were an upstanding person and how you would react to such allegations. I don't blame you at all, James, but this is completely untrue and you are the one who has been set up. You fell into their trap.'

'This is very serious,' I said. 'I have taken all these people out of your radio station and here you are, saying it is all a lie.'

'Yes,' he replied.

I wasn't satisfied with his explanation and told him I was going to look into it further. I left the radio station and walked the few doors down to Siobhan's home. Cooke had planted a seed of doubt in my mind, and probably thought I would go back and confront my colleagues. He was suggesting they had used me to set up a rival radio station, which was never the case. I was also acutely aware that the message he was giving me was also for the benefit of his new cronies who hung on his every word.

I knocked at the front door of Siobhan's house and, when her mother answered, I explained who I was. Her first response was to tell me to go away. 'I don't want to talk to you,' she said.

'I think you owe it to me to talk to me because I am after taking thirty-five people out of Cooke's radio station on the grounds that I believe something happened to your daughter there,' I told her.

Kathleen conceded and invited me into her house. I was nervous and anxious but I was following my instincts that Cooke had harmed Siobhan. I had learned about something awful and wasn't prepared to brush it under the carpet. Years later, in court, I was afraid that people might think I was some kind of nutcase, or someone with a single-minded point of view. In fact, I wasn't prepared to let it go because I believed Cooke was a bad man. It was hard to face Kathleen because I didn't even know if a priest had been to see her with regard to the tape, so I had no idea what she knew. But the whole issue of the radio station breaking up was headline news in the papers for about three days, so I knew she must have heard or read about that.

Kathleen told me she had sought help and that Siobhan had been assessed. She also confided that she too believed her daughter had been interfered with. She didn't tell me who she had been to see and I didn't believe it was my business to ask, but it did confirm to me that Cooke had abused this young girl. I left Kathleen's and marched back to Cooke's house to confront him again.

'Eamonn, it's true. You have abused a child, and as far as I am concerned, you can go on the radio and tell your lies in the newspapers, but I *know* you are a child abuser.'

From the moment I walked back into the room he had just stared at me with cold, dangerous eyes, not showing a hint of emotion. Then he said to me: 'I will see you six feet under.'

He was sitting down at the time and I leaned forward and grabbed him by the lapels of his suit jacket. The other three guys grabbed hold of me.

'Is this the way it's going to be, Eamonn?' I said. I wasn't going to hit him, but I was fuming mad. I just reacted instinctively because I was astounded by his reaction.

'You misunderstand me, James,' he continued. 'You're bringing on so many problems for yourself.'

I knew it was a threat, but I also believed I had a measure of the man. I had anticipated that he would try and intimidate me. It was a tactic he had used a lot in the past and I had witnessed it in action on other people.

From that moment on, I had no further contact with Cooke or Radio Dublin, apart from one occasion when he kerb crawled alongside me in his car at St Stephen's Green in Dublin. I was walking along the pavement and his car slowly drew up to me. There was someone in the car with him, I don't know who it was, but I just thought he was trying to impress someone.

After speaking with Siobhan's mother, I was

satisfied that Cooke was no longer abusing her daughter. That was the most important thing to me. I did, however, regret that Radio Dublin had been blown out of the water and that I had done it. At the time, I didn't see any other course of action, though, and for that reason my conscience was clear. I thought that was the end of the chapter for me, as far as the abuse was concerned, because Siobhan's family had been informed and would take whatever action they saw appropriate.

In the early-80s a book came out called *Radio Radio* and I was interviewed for the publication. I was asked about Radio Dublin and why I had acted as I did. I didn't go into details, but I said there were things about Eamonn Cooke I could never agree with and therefore I'd felt obliged to leave. Until Cooke was formally investigated and charged with child abuse offences, I didn't feel it was my right to make such serious accusations publicly, which is why I always held back from telling the whole truth, right up until I was called as a witness in his trials. When the book came out, it said that my motive for breaking up Radio Dublin had always been to set up a rival radio station and I found this incredibly frustrating and demoralising.

It wasn't until the late-90s that I once again had to face Eamonn Cooke. Detective Gerry Kelly came to my door one day and asked if he could speak to me about events in Inchicore. He didn't make accusations about Cooke because, I imagine, he didn't want to put words into my mouth. I was happy to help and told him what I knew from my days of working at Radio Dublin. I think Gerry was surprised by how clearly I remembered everything. I wasn't sure how much use I could be as a witness, but if Cooke was being investigated for allegations of abuse, I told Gerry I would help as much as I could.

I didn't sleep for several nights before the first court case. I wasn't afraid of Cooke but I was afraid I would say something that would damage the case and stop him from being convicted. I knew I just had to tell the truth and hope the jury believed my version of events. I was worried they might question my wisdom in asking teenage girls to speak to a ten year old about such delicate matters. I was a young man myself when I chose to act as I did, but even given what I know now, I still would have done the same thing. The alternative was to go and accuse Cooke without having had the chance to confirm for myself that the allegations were true. I also believe the jury accepted that I had no experience in dealing with such issues and that I just did what I could to help. The strongest feeling I experienced during the trial was one of responsibility; my greatest fear was that Cooke would try and twist my motives into something they were not.

I don't think I had any inkling about the scale of Cooke's crimes when I gave evidence during the first trial. It was Detective Gerry Kelly who pulled everything together and I believe he was the first one to realise the full horror of Cooke's abuse of children.

I gave evidence against Cooke in both his trials and was obviously delighted that he was finally convicted and jailed. I also believe that if Siobhan's family had tried to prosecute him back in the 1970s, the case would have failed because of the times we lived in. I know I am not alone in that view. Had that happened, Siobhan would not have been able to go forward as a witness as an adult and, without her, it is my belief Cooke would not have been convicted.

As far as Eamonn Cooke is concerned, he does not operate from the same moral code as ordinary, decent folk. I don't believe paedophiles like him can be cured or that counselling can work. Therefore offenders of this nature should remain locked up for the safety of society.

I thought Siobhan was incredibly brave to go through the two trials and face Cooke, and it occurred to me that his abuse of her must have been eating her up inside for decades. In many ways, it was all the more victorious for his victims that Cooke put up a fight, because right to the end he was still trying to manipulate people and he lost. He made the whole situation even harder for the witnesses by forcing them to relive their ordeals in court, and in front of him. When he was convicted no one felt sorry for the frail old man in the dock. He had lied and everyone had seen through him. He showed not an ounce of compassion for his victims and deserved none back when he was sentenced to jail.

I have no regrets about how I chose to deal with Cooke. He committed terrible crimes and had to be stopped. If I had to, I would go through it all again.

10

I never went back to Cooke's house and his abuse of me was never mentioned at home. I got on with my life as normal but I think I knew something really terrible had happened – I just didn't understand it at the time. Shortly afterwards, I can vividly remember seeing a young girl getting out of Cooke's car; she was a thin girl with straight, brown hair and not unlike me to look at. I only got a brief glimpse of her, but I knew she was one of the girls Cooke had moved on to after me. I wouldn't see her again until more than twenty years later when she came forward at his first trial. I discovered then that she had fallen pregnant to Cooke when she was a young teenager and had given birth to his son when she was fifteen. Like me, she has suffered enormous trauma throughout her life and we have now become great friends.

Feathers had been ruffled in the neighbourhood and even though Cooke had got away with his crimes, he eventually sold his house and moved to another property in Inchicore, about five minutes' walk from my home. We all breathed a silent sigh of relief. I had no idea then that the fall out from his abuse had only just begun. The physical assaults might have stopped but the psychological and emotional damage was to last most of my adult life. For now, though, while Cooke was never discussed at home, I had the constant love and reassurance of my parents.

I started secondary school at the Mater Dei Convent, also in Basin Lane. On the surface things appeared normal, but on the inside my emotions were starting to unravel. I was a good pupil and enjoyed my education, which was fairly typical of the time; nuns ran the school to a strict regime with the Church at the centre of its teaching. Once we were shown a video of an abortion and I will never forget it. We were taught about different types of abortion, the 'hoover' and the 'scraping'. Then the nun conducting the lesson read out a prayer written as if by the embryo about to be aborted. It was an anti-abortion message designed to be deliberately shocking. My parents were never asked if I could see the film; it was taken for granted then that the Church taught you what to believe.

When I was twelve, I remember a gang of us played kiss chase near my house with some of the lads we palled around with. One of the boys caught me and I tried to push him away because I didn't want to kiss him. It felt really disgusting. The boy turned to me and said, 'You can't refuse to kiss me. I know what went on with you girls and Cooke. If he can kiss you, then so can I.' Of course, Cooke had never kissed us but his words stung me like a slap in the face. My stomach turned upside down and I felt sick. It was probably the first time it dawned on me that what Cooke had done to me was wrong. It was a huge trigger point for me. I realised then that Cooke had used me. He had treated my body like a thing to do with as he wanted. I was so angry and hurt inside, but I didn't tell anyone. The shame was too great. Instead, I vowed that no bastard was ever going to touch me in that way again.

I ran away that day as fast as I could. I just wanted to get away from the boy and shut out the mocking words that were ringing in my head. I was furious and confused but I was also fearful of being exposed over what had happened in Cooke's house. I figured that if this lad knew about Cooke's abuse, then maybe other boys knew too. I was scared they would want to touch me in the same way as Cooke had. I remember I didn't cry because I didn't want to draw attention to myself or upset my parents any further. We had always played kiss chase as an innocent game but from that day it was ruined forever for me.

Shortly afterwards the father of a local boy knocked at our house and spoke to Mammy. He asked her if she was aware that her daughter had been seen playing kiss chase over at the Model School near to our house. He then added, 'I want you to know that I will not have my son playing with her again.'

There was always a group of us who played kiss chase but this man did not knock on the door of any of the other girls in our gang. I was devastated and wanted to know why he had only knocked at my door. I feared he knew what had happened to me at Cooke's and it left me feeling that I was being punished for being one of his victims. I suspected that this boy's father was afraid that I would in some way corrupt his son because of what had happened to me in the past. It had only been an innocent, childish game but it left me feeling dirty and full of shame. Mammy spoke to me about it and reassured me that I had done nothing wrong. I protected all the other girls by staying silent about their participation in the game, but once again I was shouldering the backlash to Cooke's abuse. I never played kiss chase again.

It was one further thing that left me feeling singled out and unfairly treated. But it also helped me develop a sharp sense of justice and a strong social conscience. Daddy used to have a battered blue Bedford van that lay parked outside our house for months on end because it didn't work. I used to pinch the keys and play in the back of the car with my friends. We often hid in there from the rain and played games. The smell in the back of that van would kill you. A woman in the neighbourhood was selling second-hand clothes and she asked Daddy if she could store them in the van. Some of them were so disgusting they were almost walking.

It was in this van that I used to sit with one friend who had been in Cooke's house with me. We would try and solve mysteries together and then one day we decided that we would form a detective agency when we grew up. We said we would hire our services to people who needed help in tracking down bad people. We dreamed of having cameras and tape recorders to solve people's problems. Then we said we would use our equipment to catch Cooke. We fantasised about how we would sneak into his house and spy on him or stake out his house and watch him. We wanted to take taped evidence to the police so they could arrest him and put him in jail. It was pie-in-the-sky talk, but it was a reflection of how two of his victims felt from a very young age. We didn't know then that what we really wanted was justice. We wanted him to be caught for what he had done. It was one of the rare occasions that Cooke was talked about even though the sexual abuse was never specifically mentioned.

I also remember telling my teachers at school that I wanted to become a lawyer when I grew up. Everyone else in the class just laughed at me, and I think even the teachers thought I had notions above my station. At that time, sadly, we were just seen as inner-city kids only fit to work in factories. But for me everything kept returning to this need for justice.

Although Cooke was never mentioned at home he had inflicted lasting damage on my family. On the surface Mammy and Daddy tried to keep things as normal as possible for us, but we all knew things had changed indefinably. Mammy said and did the same things as she had always done, but the bounce had disappeared from her step. As a result I felt guilty and couldn't do enough to try and please both my parents. I would go round and tidy everything up, and when I was a bit older I took to baking cakes or scones when they were out, just so I could make them happy. It was my way of saying sorry for the hurt that had been thrust upon them, which I assumed was my fault. It was only when I grew older that it also dawned on me that I was seeking their approval, a trait that Cooke had instilled in me as a little girl.

As a teenager I just wanted to feel that Mammy and Daddy still loved and trusted me, despite what had happened. They never gave me any reason to doubt their love but the damage Cooke had caused had clearly left me feeling inadequate and insecure. If anything, I received more love, and cuddles in abundance from them. They tried to ensure I had a strong sense of self and, while Cooke was never mentioned specifically, Mammy would constantly say: 'Don't ever think you are different from anyone else. Something bad happened but it was not your fault and we love you, no matter what.' It was odd because although Mammy was reassuring me, inside I was screaming because I *was* different, no matter what she said. I could also sense Mammy's silent inner torture but I didn't know how to ease the pain or how to take my guilt away. From the moment Mammy discovered how Cooke had hurt her daughter, she wanted to know where I was every minute of the day.

'I'm not being bad to you, Siobhan, but I want to know where you are going and who you are with, just so that I know that you are safe,' she would repeat like a mantra every morning.

By now Daddy had started a mobile music business – a trade I would eventually follow him into. He was selling singles, LPs and cassette tapes around the country at various markets. When the school holidays came around, he asked if I wanted to go with him and I jumped at the chance. I relished every moment of it even though we had to get up painfully early every morning to travel for miles to the different venues. It was a great bonding exercise between Daddy and me, and we became very close. Of course both my parents were relieved I was with him because then they could be sure that I was safe. The only way they could guarantee I was protected was when I was with my daddy. It also got me out of Inchicore at a very unsettled time in our lives.

I loved the whole experience, moving around the country and discovering new places for the first time. It gave me my enduring love of Irish music. I would spend the summers on the road and it was a great distraction which meant I didn't dwell on Cooke. There were also our family holidays in Galway still, therapy in themselves.

I don't think I was ever seriously jealous of my siblings but I did feel differently towards them after Cooke abused me. There were the ordinary squabbles between us about who had to do the muckiest chores around the house and I was always envious of my sister Adrienne's gorgeous figure. I didn't have the greatest self-esteem to start with but Adrienne always seemed to look lovely and I would peer in the mirror and see myself as the ugly duckling of the family by contrast. It didn't help that she was naturally tall and willowy with a lovely slender body while I was short and ordinary. She would sometimes pinch my clothes to wear and I could never fathom why they looked so different on her. She always looked amazing yet when I wore the same outfit I looked dowdy and frumpy.

But if I felt jealous of anything about my siblings it was of their total innocence, and there was nothing I could ever do to regain mine. It wasn't that I wished something bad would happen to them, I just wished it hadn't happened to me. As a teenager, meeting young boys for the first time, I was in the sorry position of knowing what last base was before I had even got to first. I was grateful that my brothers and sister still had their innocence but I wished with all my might I still had mine, and hated Cooke for depriving me of a natural adolescence.

I was also very protective towards all my siblings and in many ways became their third parent. Like Mammy and Daddy, I wanted to know they were safe.

'If anyone hurts you, you must tell me,' I drilled into them constantly.

I was trying to protect everyone, from my brothers and sister to Mammy and Daddy because I didn't want any of my family to be hurt anymore.

I have no recollection of it, but Adrienne remembers an incident after Cooke had stopped abusing me. She says that I saw a young girl going into his garage, followed her in and dragged her out by the hair. Adrienne is a year and nine months younger than me but she also recalls a sense of something being wrong in our house around that time. She knew Mammy and Daddy changed then but she didn't know how or why. She remembers hearing Mammy crying and realising that she was heartbroken. She kept asking me what had gone on but I would just repeat: 'Nothing, nothing, nothing.' She was always quieter than me but has since confided in me that the insecurity she experienced then left her fearful and anxious and made her withdrawn. They were desperate times but our family pulled together in the best way we knew how and we survived.

As my body began to develop into a young woman's, I started to wear baggy and unflattering clothes. I cut my hair short and acted like a real tomboy so that none of the boys would notice me as a girl. I was full of self-disgust and anger but I bottled everything up because I didn't really understand my own feelings. It was a very lonely place to be.

I had learned that it was wrong for Cooke to have touched me, but I didn't know why it was wrong. I had never heard the words paedophile or pervert and continually questioned what had happened. *If no one is supposed to touch my private parts, then why did Mr Cooke do it to me?* I wondered.

Worse still, I also began to question why I'd *allowed* him to do it.

The girls at school had begun to talk about boys and what they looked like naked. It was a normal part of adolescence, but I was terrified they would find out I was different from them because I had already seen a naked man in a state of arousal. Once again, I was keeping secret the truth about Cooke and his abuse of me. Deep shame swept through me because I knew I shouldn't already understand such things. It was like I had two people in my head. *Why did you let him? Why did you let him?* I kept ranting to myself. I told myself that I should have known better, when of course I couldn't have done because I was just an innocent child.

Ever the tomboy, I joined an athletics club and loved it. I would go running at events staged all over the country. I would train during the week and then go off to trials at the weekends. I will never forget one particular athletics trip to Germany. After playing our sport, us girls went to get showered and changed. To our shock, there was a communal shower in the changing rooms and so all the Irish girls went in it and got washed in their swimsuits or their underwear. We were so prudish, I think we would rather have died than share a shower with other naked women. We had so much shame about nudity and our own bodies, but were fascinated by the newly liberated young German women who were entirely comfortable about being naked around one another. They in turn thought we were hilarious for refusing to take our undergarments off in the shower.

I made a lot of male friends through the athletics club and was comfortable around them so long as they saw me as one of the lads. I didn't want to feel or be treated as feminine or to have any of the boys look at me. In my head I could still hear Cooke saying, 'You're my special girl.' I had experienced that sort of attention already and I didn't like it. I never wanted to go back there again.

When I was thirteen, we went on a school trip to Belgium. All the girls' bodies were starting to grow and change. My bust was starting to develop and I remember one of the girls saying to me, 'Siobhan Kennedy, you need a bra because you can see your nipples through your top.' I didn't feel uncomfortable at her 'skitting' me because she didn't know about what had happened at Cooke's house. I liked being away from home and around my school friends because, with them, my past remained a secret. I could believe I was as fresh and undamaged as they were. In their minds, I was the same as them. I just didn't feel like it on the inside.

But I was constantly filled with fear and dread that they would one day discover I was different. How would they look at me if they knew what I had done and what Cooke had done to me? I wanted more than anything to be normal like them; not to have to carry this terrible secret around with me. I was terrified that if any of the boys got word that I had let a man put his hand down my knickers, they might want to do the same thing and then I would get a bad name. Being called a slut was the worst insult anyone could throw at you. It was what girls would shout at one another if they got into a fight, and I was scared that if my friends knew about Cooke they would called me the biggest slut of all. That was my secret dread. I felt ashamed and dirty just thinking about it.

When I returned from the school trip, Mammy took me to be measured for my first bra. We received some sex education in school but it was pretty damned useless. Typical of a Catholic education, nuns took the sex education lessons. They didn't tell you that you had sex because you enjoyed it or because you were in love with someone. As far as they were concerned, you only had sex to reproduce the human race. It was more like a biology lesson and there was no mention of arousal, excitement or pleasure so we learned nothing of the emotional aspect of sex. We were shown a diagram of male and female reproductive organs. The message was: 'Here's the ovaries, here's the vagina. If the penis is inserted into the vagina and releases sperm that meets the egg, then you have a baby. If the egg is not fertilised, you have a period.' That was our sex education in a nutshell. I didn't understand about penetration and was overcome with a feeling of panic as I thought to myself, *Oh God, have I had sex then?* I was filled with horror and felt soiled and tawdry.

I started my periods and Mammy showed me how to use a sanitary towel. Everything was fine for the first day because I understood what was happening, but when the blood didn't stop for five days, I thought I was bleeding to death. No one had told me it would last more than a day and I was too afraid to tell anyone. My school friends were obsessed by three topics – periods, boobs and pubes. They also wanted to know who had got their first 'ware', which was the slang terminology for a full on kiss or a snog. In my mind, I kept thinking, *Jaysus, if they only knew what I have already done.* I had no boobs to speak of and I'd not yet had my first ware, but I had experienced a man with his head and his erection between my legs! I was really struggling to understand it all and tried desperately to rationalise it over and over in my head.

Although I had cripplingly low self esteem, in my heart I still always believed I was a good person who knew the difference between right and wrong. I also wanted to help people who were in trouble. I think this is because I myself knew what it was like to be troubled. I was trying to prove myself and find ways to make myself a better person because I still felt guilty that I had allowed Cooke to abuse me. Nothing at that time could have convinced me it was not my fault.

When I was fourteen, I joined the Peace Corps in Ballyfermot. It was run by the Catholic Church and I would go to the parochial house with a friend I shall call Jack. He was extremely effeminate and I was very fond of him. Father Michael Cleary and Father Tony Walsh lived in the parish house at that time, and one day Father Walsh came up behind me and started massaging my shoulders. I instantly felt repulsed and physically sick at his touch, and pulled away from him.

'What are you doing?' I asked him.

'Just giving you a little massage,' he replied.

'I don't like it, don't touch me,' I snapped back. With that I left the house.

His touch had made me cringe and I immediately compared it with Cooke's. Father Walsh gave me the creeps. I now knew this sort of contact was wrong. I hadn't realised with Cooke but now that I was older it was different. Jack was regularly in that parish house but if Father Walsh abused him, he never confided in me. Not long after Walsh was convicted as a paedophile, my old friend was found dead in England. I remember being so sad when I heard that news because until then I'd had no idea what had become of Jack or what had happened in his life.

A short while after the incident at Ballyfermot, Daddy came home one day and told us all he was arranging for a Mass to be said at our house to mark the anniversary of Gran's death. He said that Father Walsh was taking the Mass. As quick as a flash, I said I wouldn't attend the service. It was the first time I had ever defied my daddy.

'Why don't you want to attend Mass?' he asked.

'Because I don't like Father Walsh,' I replied stubbornly.

When he asked me why not, I answered, 'Because I don't.'

It caused uproar in our house but when I saw Walsh it was the same for me as looking at Cooke. For some reason I seemed to have a sixth sense about a man who at this stage had not been accused of any sex crimes against children. Call it intuition, but I knew from a very early age he could not be trusted and my instincts proved to be right.

By the time I reached the age of fifteen, the New Romantics and Duran Duran were the height of fashion. My favourite song was 'Don't You Want Me Baby', by a band called The Human League. I remember a school pal called Brenda who came into class one day with her hair cut into a complete V-shape, just like the band members in The Human League. She was thrown out of school, but I thought she looked amazing.

We started going to school discos and I began to dress up a little bit more because I didn't want to feel left out. I had always been into jeans and baggy tops but now I wanted to be a little more fashionable. I was comfortable with boys so long as I didn't have to be anyone's girlfriend. I knew now that Cooke had used me and I never wanted that to happen again. I made a pact with myself that no one would ever use me again, and I would only get close to a lad if I really wanted to be with him.

We went on another school trip and this time it was to London. We went over on the boat and I got chatting to a lad called Paul who was seventeen. He told me that he had joined the army and was a mechanic. We had a lovely chat and got on really well. Paul asked if I would write to him and I agreed. He then asked me for a kiss goodbye and I nearly froze on the spot. I had practised a million times by kissing mirrors and the back of my hand but this was the real thing and I was petrified. I tried to be sophisticated and grown up but I got the shock of my life when his tongue went into my mouth. I had got my first 'ware'! I was surprised to find I enjoyed the sensation and was pretty pleased with myself. Eventually I went back to my friends and told them about Paul. They were laughing and pressed me for all the details. My first proper kiss had been a normal and natural experience.

I felt very 'girlie' for the first time in years and briefly enjoyed being the centre of everyone's attention. I was happy and felt that I finally fitted in. I finally believed I belonged with these other teenage girls on our shared, normal adolescent journey of discovery. But the feeling was short-lived because underneath my excitement and giggling moment of joy I harboured the dark reality of my past. I still couldn't escape the fact that I knew my outlook on these experiences was different because I had already experienced sexual contact far beyond a 'ware'. Cooke had deprived me of the pleasures of a normal rite of passage from child to adult.

Back in Inchicore, I wrote to Paul for a little while but in the end it fizzled out. But meeting him had shifted something inside me. I wanted to embrace the changes that my friends and I were going through. I asked my mum if I could buy a skirt and blouse to wear to discos. She took me shopping and I got a green and white ra-ra skirt and a green v-neck top to match. I wore little white shoes to complete the look and thought I looked the bee's knees. Until then, I had worn jeans, a granddad shirt and a purple jumper every week. The jumper was so worn it even had an iron mark on the back. The lads got a big shock when they saw me dressed up for the first time. I had never been interested in making the most of myself before.

I was slim and short with fair hair and freckles. Just an average-looking girl. There was nothing spectacular about me; I didn't have gorgeous hair or perfect teeth or sparkling eyes. I remember there were some really good-looking girls in my school at the time, and yet the boys liked to be around me. None of my friends could understand this, but the boys would tell me it was because I never got embarrassed or blushed around them. I was always more like a mate.

That year, we decided we would all try and get into a pub for a drink. It was in June on the night of the last school dance before the summer holidays. I certainly didn't look eighteen, but some of the girls knew which were the lenient pubs from listening to their older sisters. First off, we scraped all our money together and went to a supermarket. Outside we persuaded a local alcoholic to buy us some booze in return for a few drinks for himself. Three of us shared a six-pack of Stag cider and drank two bottles each. By the time we had drunk them, we were all flying and oozing with confidence. We walked down the forty steps to Bow Lane in Dublin and found a pub that would serve us drinks without any questions. That night I had my first vodka and orange juice. All six of us ordered the same drink. If that wasn't a giveaway that we were buying drinks in a pub for the first time, I don't know what was, but the barman served us all the same. We only had enough money for one drink in the pub but it was enough because we were not used to alcohol and as we had already drunk the cider beforehand it immediately had the desired effect.

We made our way back to the disco at the Christian Brothers School in Inchicore. I felt brilliant with the alcohol inside me and I was in great humour. I felt like I had never felt before, as if relief and happiness were sweeping over me like a wave. I completely forgot about the demons that nagged away inside me. All my bad thoughts seemed to evaporate and I felt liberated. The boys in the disco sussed that us girls had been drinking and capitalised on it. One lad asked me up to dance and I felt so bold I snogged him on the dance floor. It wouldn't have happened if I had not had a drink.

This was my first introduction to alcohol and as far as I was concerned it was something you took to make you enjoy yourself and forget all your problems. When I drank, it made me feel that nothing mattered; I felt alive instead of paranoid that my friends knew my dark secret. I normally felt so ashamed inside. How could I ever tell my friends what I had let Cooke do to me? They would surely hate me if they knew. Alcohol got rid of those awful feelings for me. I also felt a new sense of belonging with my friends because we had all shared something together for the first time.

I didn't spend much time with my old friends back home because I was so busy with school and athletics. When we did hang out, for those of us who had played at Cooke's house there was an unspoken rule that we never mentioned him or what had happened to us. It was a silent but mutual understanding between us. None of us wanted to confront what we had been through together. It was as if, by ignoring it, we could somehow pretend it had never happened. We knew we were different from other kids but if we buried the pain deep enough we could try and pretend the horrors of our childhood had happened to different people or that they were just a terrible nightmare. The last time Cooke had been mentioned by the whole group was when we'd huddled by the telegraph pole outside my house, plotting our escape.

I still couldn't shake the fear that my friends in school would find out what he had done to me. I was so scared they would shun me if they ever learned the truth and I knew this went back to when some of my old friends had told me they could not play with me anymore. I was desperate to be liked and accepted by the girls. (I didn't care about the boys and perhaps that is why I got on with them so much better.) I was determined not to be an outcast again like I was when I was ten. I spent all my energy trying to cover up my past and blend in as far as possible. I never wanted to feel like a freak again.

I carried on wearing nice clothes so that I felt the same as the other girls but I hated it when boys made comments about me, like, 'Doesn't Siobhan Kennedy look well? I never knew she had boobs.'

It made me feel very self-conscious and uncomfortable that they were looking at my body. I kept worrying that if they thought I looked nice, they would want to touch me. So in the end I stopped wearing dresses and skirts and went back to jeans and tops. Because I assumed boys were only interested in boobs I hid my bust once again inside a baggy granddad shirt. My friends, meanwhile, were trying hard to show off their assets by squeezing their boobs up and wearing tight tops. All the same, I decided once and for all that skirts, dresses and make-up were not for me; if people didn't accept me the way I was then they could forget it. I hated the attention that dressing up brought, and seeing myself looking so attractive and girly had also dredged up memories of my childhood I didn't want to face. I associated dressing up with wearing skirts which took me back to dancing in Cooke's garden that very first summer. How could I try to forget all that if just looking in the mirror reminded me of the innocent little girl I once was?

I wanted to join in the *craic* with my pals, but sexually I wanted to be invisible. I wanted to be liked for my personality, not just because I had a pair of boobs or wore a tight blouse. The girls in school just laughed at sex education but I didn't think it was funny because I knew what lay ahead for them. I still thought of sex as a bad thing because it had happened to me at the wrong time, as a child and not a young adult. When some of the girls confided they had started having sex, I just froze inside and became even more frightened of attracting the opposite sex. My friends told me that you couldn't let anyone touch you unless you really loved them, otherwise the boys would think you were easy. It was torment for me and I knew I was never going to let the boys pass me around like a toy. I hoped that one day I might meet someone special. I knew I would have to tell him about Cooke, but I wanted him to love me first. I knew all the boys I was friends with were nowhere near mature enough to handle all this.

Something else that I held sacred was my belief in God's love for me. But Cooke's actions had jeopardised even that. The Catholic Church dictated that you were not supposed to have sex outside of marriage and I felt certain that what I'd allowed Cooke to do was just as sinful. So I began to feel scared that God didn't love me anymore because Cooke had touched me. I begged Him to forgive me for what someone else had done to me as a child. I kept trying to explain to Him in my prayers that I didn't know what I was doing. The idea that I was unlovable terrified me and I was consumed with fear at the prospect of a future without even God's love.

Throughout my teenage years, it was almost impossible for me to form proper intimate relationships. As friends around me started dating boys, I couldn't bring myself to let anyone touch me or even come near me. Other girls who were abused by Cooke acted differently. I have since spoken with a lot of women who have suffered sexual abuse, not just by Cooke, and it seems they tend to adopt one of two patterns of behaviour. There are the women who withdraw and refuse to allow men to come anywhere near them, and then there are those who sleep with lots of men, older men or married men, because they feel their bodies are so badly violated already that it will make no difference to them anyway. I know I shared that same self-disgust with my body but I responded by refusing to let anyone get physically intimate with me. Cooke had stolen my childhood innocence and now the silent scars of his abuse had ravaged my adolescence. Would I ever feel normal? Could I ever escape the demons of my past?

11

On the day after my sixteenth birthday I started a summer
holiday job at St James's Hospital in Dublin. In due course I
wanted to become a nurse, as I wanted to care for people, so
it was the perfect opportunity to see if I was cut out for
hospital work. This was a new and exciting experience for
me, earning a wage in the adult world for the first time. I was
extremely proud of my job and worked very hard at it. I
started on the geriatric ward, helping out the nurses and
running errands for the staff. I didn't see much of my friends
that summer because most of us had part time jobs by this
stage. We were also starting to grow out of spending our free
time just hanging around the streets in a gang.

It was just another normal day at work when I was
suddenly confronted by the face of my nightmares. I'd been
working on the Intensive Care Unit when I was completely
knocked sideways by the sight of Eamonn Cooke lying asleep
or unconscious in one of the beds. My first thought was, *I hope
you die, you bastard, I hope you never wake up again.* I felt hysterical
inside but tried to remain outwardly calm. My head was
racing and I felt sick to my stomach as I focussed on him. He

was hooked up to lots of drips and wires and I looked around me to see who was about. Then I was gripped by an urge to go and rip every plug and drip from his body and smother his face with a pillow. I began to fantasise about how my mop might accidentally become wrapped around his tubes and pull them out and kill him. I realised that for the first time I had real power over him. Here was the man who had tried to destroy so many innocent lives, lying unconscious in a bed before me. He was defenceless, just as I had been as a child. My emotions were in tumult. I felt fear, anger, and then jubilation that maybe payback day had finally arrived. If he was in Intensive Care, I reasoned, then there was a good chance he might die. Would God mind if I helped him on his way?

I looked at his sleeping face and then that body that haunted my nightmares, and I felt ill. I wanted to scream at him, *You have no fucking idea what you have done to me or my family!* I felt that it was so unjust that all these nurses and doctors were trying to save the life of a man who had harmed so many, a man who didn't deserve to live. I wondered how the medics would feel about saving his life if they knew what a monster Cooke really was? I even questioned God. *Why do all the good people die while the bad bastards seem to live? Can you not just take him out now and spare us all a load of misery?* I begged. I even considered stabbing Cooke with a knife from the hospital kitchen.

In the end, I did absolutely nothing but walk up to his bedside and peer down into his oblivious face. 'See you, you evil bastard. I hope you rot in hell,' I spat before I walked away with my head held high.

I don't know what prevented me from harming him that day, but something made me realise that two wrongs do not make a right. The sooner everyone in this world realises that, the sooner it will be a better place to live in. I don't think I would have been able to live with myself if I had hurt or killed Cooke that day, even though I am sure God would have understood why I did it. I had had the power to harm him, but had chosen not to exercise it. It turned my stomach when I looked at him to think that any part of that body had been anywhere near mine, especially looking at his mouth and thinking, *Oh my God, what did you do to me as a child?* I'd felt complete revulsion and been tempted to take my revenge on him, but my faith in God proved stronger than my anger. When I go to meet my Maker, I want to have a clear conscience; which is something Cooke will never be able to have.

I still hated him with a passion, of course, and asked my manager if I could be transferred to another ward. I couldn't bear to be around him. I also didn't trust myself not to lose my cool in a moment of rage and go back on that decision not to harm him. Just the sight of him made it hard for me to control my emotions.

When I heard that he had survived I was profoundly disturbed and also angry with God. I don't know what His masterplan for Cooke is on this earth, but I do know if ever my own faith was tested it was during this episode. If I had killed him then, I could have saved myself a whole lot of the torment that lay ahead for me because of him. If I had helped him slip away that day countless kids might have been spared from abuse, and I would definitely have been spared the ordeal of testifying in two trials. But if I had committed murder I don't know if I could have lived with the guilt. Maybe God's plan was to ensure I lived to see justice served on my abuser after all.

Not long after I saw Cooke at the hospital, I started to date a boy I will call Jason. I think I felt I needed to take back some control of my life, and seeing my tormentor had finally made me realise I also needed to take some risks otherwise he'd have won. I met Jason through some friends when I was sixteen and he was two years older than me. I thought he was really mature and he made me feel good about myself. I was also sure he liked me for the person I was and not because he was seeking some cheap sexual favour. He had a bubbly personality like mine and was considerate and kind. He sent me little cards with love letters inside and would take me out on dates for a proper steak meal. I was impressed and began to feel like a grown up for the first time. We dated for several months and yet all I'd allowed him to do to me was to kiss me. I couldn't face the idea of taking it any further with him or any man. I was feeling quite confused because I felt I loved Jason but I was still too scared to commit to a physical relationship. I knew that if I had sex it had to be with a man I'd marry and live with the rest of my life. I know these beliefs were partly because of my religious upbringing, but I think Cooke's abuse of me was an even stronger factor in determining my behaviour because I was so adamant that I never wanted to be used just for sex by a man again.

I left school at seventeen with my leaving certificates and my parents were very proud of me. They weren't pushy parents who insisted I become a high-flying career woman.

Their attitude had always remained the same: that so long as I was healthy and happy and lived a good life they would be proud of me, regardless of what I chose to do. Shortly after my seventeenth birthday, Jason proposed to me and I said yes. We declared how much we loved each other but still he didn't try and push me into having sex until I was ready. We were deliriously happy, but my parents weren't quite so chuffed. They kept telling me to slow down, that I had my whole life ahead of me, but I thought I was in love with Jason and that I knew best. Daddy thought I was too young even to be talking about getting married. I didn't care how old I was because this was really the first time in my life I'd felt confident and pretty as a young woman. I even dressed up a bit more in skirts and high heels, and this boost in confidence was all down to my relationship with Jason and the trust I could place in him.

One summer's evening, short of money but wanting to enjoy some time alone, Jason and I went on a camping trip together, and this was when I had my first consensual and loving sexual experience. We were on our own together for the first time and I felt really relaxed and happy with him. It was very special, but sadly the experience also made me realise the full extent of Cooke's sexual crimes against me. I couldn't hide how upset and shaken I was by the realisation and Jason was very worried about me so, slowly but surely, I began to tell him what had happened to me. He wasn't surprised and told me that he had always suspected something like that because of the way I'd held back from sex. I didn't tell him many details and he didn't push me either.

Around this time, I changed my mind about wanting to become a nurse. I had been transferred to work on a bone marrow transplant unit on a cancer ward. My job was to scrub everything as clean as was humanly possible to make sure it was ultra-hygienic. I befriended a young girl on the ward who told me she had cysts on her ovaries. The reality, I knew, was that she was riddled with cancer. I became quite emotionally attached to this sick young girl and found I was having nightmares about her when I went to sleep. One day I went into work and her bed was empty. She had died and I felt quite devastated, although really I had barely known her. I found it so upsetting and difficult to deal with that I didn't feel I could be a good nurse. It was a difficult decision but in the end I left the hospital and went to work in a chemist's instead.

But overall it was a happy time in my life, especially once I settled into my new job. I loved Jason and we had such fun, going to parties together and making new friends. Life was finally feeling good despite the turmoil I still suffered inside. I thought I was doing well at hiding it; at being as normal as I could be. Little did I know how much things were to change for the worse.

Not long after leaving St James's Hospital, I read a newspaper article about Eamonn Cooke. The story reported his involvement in the petrol bombing of a house. Cooke had been behind an arson attack on the home of a young man who had started dating one of his former victims. She was now a young woman herself, but years earlier she was one of the girls Cooke had moved on to after he'd stopped abusing me. After she had given birth to his son, she tried to get away from Cooke but he had taken his revenge on her by fire bombing the home of her new boyfriend. It was the first time I'd realised how violent he could be; it was also the first time, as an adult, that I became really afraid of Cooke. I read the article over and over and it totally changed my perception of him. I had always known he was bad for abusing me as he had. But this was the first time I felt real fear, because now I knew he was capable of hurting my family and me, should I ever give him reason to.

In 1986 I discovered that I was pregnant which was a huge shock. My first reaction was, *How on earth am I going to tell Mammy and Daddy?* Then I started worrying once again what people were going to think of me. Would they call me names and think I was a slut? It was the same old story, just a different set of circumstances. Abortion was not something I would consider because of my religious beliefs but there were no unmarried mothers in my area so I felt enormous shame and self-doubt. Jason was very supportive at the time but I knew Mammy was going to freak out, whichever way I put it to her. I decided to tell my maternal gran first. I arranged to have lunch with her and went over to see her. I was so anxious I didn't know what to do with myself, but as it turned out Gran made everything very easy for me.

As soon as I got there she said, 'Siobhan, have you got something to tell me? Because I'm over at your house every week, and as far as I can make out you've stopped drinking tea, which to me is a sure sign of pregnancy.'

She could have knocked me down with a feather! Gran had guessed before I even had the chance to tell her.

'You're not the first and you won't be the last. So long as

you and the baby are fine, that's all I care about, and I am sure your mother and father will agree with me. Don't worry what anyone else thinks,' she told me. I was so relieved and reassured by Gran's response, but then she delivered her knockout punch. 'I'm giving you two weeks to tell your mammy or else I will tell her myself.'

I knew I had no choice and so a few nights later, when I returned home from work, I blurted it all out to Mammy.

'I'm going to have a baby – and before you say anything, Gran already knows so you don't have to worry about what she thinks.'

'Oh my God!' Mammy replied. 'Don't tell your father, I'll speak to him myself about this.'

Mammy was understandably shocked but she was also very supportive of me. Later on, when I was in bed, I heard her telling Daddy the news and he was very upset. That obviously upset me also, but at least both my parents now knew.

The next day when I got up Daddy came and spoke to me. 'Siobhan, there's not much I can say to you, but I do love you and I do care about you very much. Your mammy loves you too. We will get through this, as a family, together. I can't say I'm not disappointed or heartbroken for you because I know how hard this will be for a young woman,' he said to me softly, and with that I knew things would be OK. There was no speech or lecture about shame, or how the neighbours were going to react, and I was so grateful for that. Both Mammy and Daddy were there for me and that felt good. Daddy also advised me not to go through with the wedding to Jason until I was certain it was the right thing to do. It helped a lot to know they didn't want to pressure me into marriage.

My baby was due in October 1986, and between February and August that year Jason went off to England to study and work. He would return sporadically at weekends and during breaks from his commitments across the water. I remember him coming back in August 1986 because I had a hospital appointment, which we attended together. I was suffering from pre-eclampsia and they took me into hospital that day where I remained until our baby was born.

Things had changed between Jason and me, especially when he moved to England. My parents couldn't understand why he had given up a job in Ireland when I was pregnant but I think he was trying to build us a better future. Either way, it's fair to say the honeymoon period between us was well and truly over.

My first son Glenn* was born prematurely in September by emergency Caesarian section, weighing five pounds and thirteen ounces. I loved him instantly and was relieved that he was okay after the difficult pregnancy. Eventually I took Glenn home but by then I had changed as a person. I felt wholly responsible for this defenceless little bundle and he became the most important thing in my life. I was still living at home but put my name down with the local authority to get a place of our own. Before long, I was offered a lovely two-bedroomed flat in Inchicore and accepted it. My parents were beside themselves. I was nineteen years old, and about to go and live on my own with a new baby. They begged me to stay

* : name changed.

but I really needed my own space so I could bring up my baby in the way I thought best. Things had deteriorated with Jason and there was a sense of distance between us. He visited Glenn and me at the new flat, but our relationship was over and we both knew it. When Glenn was seven months old, Jason and I finally went our separate ways. We were both so young. Now my only priority in life was taking care of my baby. I dedicated myself to looking after him.

I hadn't been living in the flat for very long when a friend of mine from Inchicore came to see me. She had been one of the girls Cooke had abused at the same time as me. She told me she was going to go to the Garda and make a statement against him, and asked if I would go with her.

I wanted to help her but was too frightened to come forward at that time. My son was all I could think about and I was still very frightened of Cooke. I often looked at Glenn and saw how vulnerable he was. I couldn't understand how any man could hurt a child in any way, and it made me want to protect Glenn even more. If I hadn't had a young baby to consider, I might have gone with her to the police but it's hard to be certain now. She went on her own anyway and informed the Garda for the first time of Cooke's abuse of young children. I greatly admired her courage and resolve but it was in vain as nothing came of her statement. At least she had tried, though, even if at that time others didn't come forward to back her up. It must have taken a lot for her to go and see the police and tell them what she had suffered. I will never forget her bravery.

Since Glenn had been born, I had hardly been out and so one night Mammy looked after him so I could relax and enjoy an evening with friends. I had forgotten what it was like to have fun. After that, I went out occasionally, whenever a relative was happy to baby-sit. The rest of the time, I just looked after my son. It wasn't always easy on my own but I was content. In my own simple way, I built a little home for the two of us to share and Glenn remained the centre of my world. There were no boyfriends on the scene. If I went out for an evening, I might allow a gentleman to walk me home, but anything more was out of the question. It just wasn't something I could contemplate after my break-up with Jason. For now I was content being single and looking after Glenn.

12

The week after I celebrated my twenty-first birthday in May 1988, I met the man who was to change my life forever. I went out for the evening in Dublin with some friends. We got chatting to another group and I got on particularly well with one of the men. At the end of the night he asked me if I would meet him next week in a bar called Coopers in O'Connell Street in the centre of the city. That man was Derek, and little did I know then that he was the one I would eventually marry. I agreed to meet him with absolutely no intention of turning up because I still couldn't even consider getting involved in a relationship. But I told my sister about him, and she sensed that I liked him. So when the following week came around, she persuaded me to go and meet him.

When I arrived at Coopers, I saw Derek immediately and he came up to greet me. He thanked me for coming then he introduced me to about ten of his friends. I nearly fainted. It was bad enough meeting one person you didn't really know, but I was thrown in at the deep end, meeting a huge crowd of his friends all at once. It turned out to be a brilliant evening. They were all very nice and made me feel relaxed and comfortable. At the end of the evening, Derek asked me if he could take me on a proper date. I said he could, then added I would have to bring my son. It was the first time I had mentioned to Derek that I had a child. He didn't flinch but when I turned up to meet him on the next date, with Glenn in tow, he looked a bit surprised. He had thought I was only joking when I said I had a baby, but we all went out for the day anyway.

It was a big test for me because I had never introduced my son to anyone but family and close friends before now. Derek took it all in his stride, though. The next time he took us both out, we were sitting on a bus and the baby was jabbering away as babies do. An old lady sitting next to us turned and said, 'Oh, look at you, with your lovely family. Isn't your son just the image of his daddy?' I nearly died. Sensing Derek's alarm at what the woman had said, I thought I was never going to see this chap again, but he surprised me by arranging another date. The following week he took us both out for coffee and a burger and we just talked, gradually getting to know one another.

A few weeks went by and Derek stuck around. He was a perfect gentleman and treated my son and me so well. I thought he was wonderful. Not many men would have wanted to take on a young girl with a baby, but Derek was different.

One day he told me that his friend had joined the Navy and his passing out parade was taking place in Cork the coming weekend. He apologised for the short notice, but asked if I wanted to go with him and his friends. I knew the pals he was going with and they were a nice group of people.

My initial response was to say no because I immediately thought he would want to share a room with me. I also thought Mammy would be unimpressed if I wanted to go away with a man I hadn't known that long. And there was no way I could go without her knowing because naturally I would have to ask her to look after Glenn. There I was, twenty-one years of age, still asking my parents' permission to go away for the weekend with my boyfriend! But I really liked Derek and felt very comfortable with him. I finally got up the courage to speak to Mammy about it, and although she didn't think it was a good idea, she still agreed to look after Glenn. It wasn't until the day before we travelled that I rang Derek and said I would love to go with him. He was delighted.

The following day six of us squashed into a VW Beetle and drove down to Cork for the weekend. When we arrived at the hotel, I was gripped with fear because I had said nothing to Derek about our sleeping arrangements. To my amazement, he had booked us separate rooms and I was thrilled. It showed that he respected me and liked me for the person I was. We all spent two nights in a bed and breakfast but on the final night couldn't find anywhere to stay. In the end Derek and I were forced to sleep in the car, but when we woke up in the morning I nearly died of embarrassment. All these people in their Sunday best were walking past the car, wagging their fingers and 'tutting' at us in disgust. Derek had parked outside a church without thinking and now all the parishioners going to the half-seven Mass were walking past, looking at his feet sticking up by the window. I was mortified but an hour later we were creased up with laughter as we drove home to Dublin. When we arrived at my flat, I invited him in for the first time.

After that Derek became a permanent fixture in my life and made me very happy and contented. He never asked questions about my past but gradually I volunteered information about my relationship with Jason. Derek and I had kissed and cuddled during our trip to Cork, but as yet had not gone any further. We got to know each other's family and friends, and gradually I fell in love with him. Derek included Glenn in everything we did, and I think we both knew early on that our feelings were heading in the same direction. He also knew I had suffered a bad experience in my life, but didn't pry.

Derek was planning to join the Navy like his friend and after his initial interview had to go through a medical with his doctor. I went with him and took Glenn along too. As it was with his local GP, we pretended Glenn was my baby brother, even though he kept calling me 'Mammy'. We hadn't told Derek's mother that I had a child and I didn't want her to find out through local gossip.

A few days after that, Derek was having a shave at home when his mam Peggy turned to him and said, 'How's it going, son?'

'Fine,' he replied.

'Well, the doctor says that if Siobhan's son wants the bike he was playing with down at the surgery, he can have it because his children have finished with it.'

With that she walked off and Derek nearly slit his throat with his razor in shock. It was her way of telling her son that she knew I had a child, and I really respected and loved her for that. Shortly afterwards I took Glenn to meet her and she couldn't have made us feel more welcome. She was so warm and gentle with us both, and I am still close to her today. I could easily see where Derek got his caring nature from.

In August 1988 he joined the Navy and was moved down to Cork for recruitment training. Every Sunday evening I would go to see his mother and we would both speak to Derek on the telephone. When he passed out, I travelled to Cork with his family to watch him and it was a very proud day for us all.

Our relationship progressed at a slow and easy pace. Derek made me feel very special. I felt loved and cherished as never before. For the first time, I didn't associate a physical relationship with the bad things that had happened to me with Cooke. When I felt ready to tell Derek more about my childhood, I explained to him that a neighbour had hurt me when I was a child, touching me, and a lot of other children, in an inappropriate way. It helped him to understand why I had been so slow and cautious in starting our relationship. Bu then, I'd never felt safer and happier. Derek's deep love for me eased some of the hurt I had suffered in my early life.

We became engaged on Christmas Eve that same year – just seven months after we had met – and everyone was shocked because we hadn't been together very long. But for the first time I didn't feel I needed anyone else's approval or blessing. Derek and I knew we wanted to be together, and nothing was going to stop us. I was still twenty-one and he was twenty-two. We went shopping together and I picked out an engagement ring then we went home to see my parents. I told them I had become engaged and, although they liked Derek, they seemed worried that it was too soon. I realised Derek was going away with the Navy but I had a huge amount of trust in him. I knew he would never let me down. I'd told him there were two rules in our relationship: 'You never hit me, and you never go with another woman,' which Derek accepted. My parents remained wary at first, worried that I was going to be hurt again, but in time they came around to the idea and grew to like him immensely.

I found it hard when Derek was away with his job, but when he was home life was wonderful. He brought Glenn up as his own and always treated us both brilliantly. On the day we became engaged, he told me: 'I love you and your son equally.' I knew he meant it because he showed it to us all the time. I was delighted that Derek cared so much for my child, but had made up my mind from early on that I would never deny Glenn the right to know his biological father.

Glenn had always called Derek by his name, and when he was about four he started asking questions about his natural father. He wanted to know if he was adopted and I was a bit unsure as to what I should say. Gran, however, knew exactly how to respond. One day she took two plants and placed them on a piece of newspaper. She divided the plants and joined two clumps together in a new pot. She said to Glenn, 'I have covered the roots with soil, but when you go home, you are going to take this pot with you and you will be responsible for keeping it alive and healthy. You have to water it and keep it in a nice warm place, and I want you to tell me from time to time how the plant is growing. It's not the person who plants the seed that is important, it's the person who feeds it, loves and nurtures it who will make it grow big and strong and happy.'

In her own way, Gran had just explained to Glenn that while he had a biological father, like every other child, it was Derek who cared for him and it was Derek he could rely on to be there for him.

'So does that mean that Derek is like my dad, Gran?' asked my son.

'Yes,' she said, and from that day on he called Derek 'dad' and no matter what ordinary family rows they have had over the years, he has never gone back on that decision. That plant is still alive and thriving today. We call it Glenn's plant. It is huge and is deeply symbolic of the love that has flourished between Derek and Glenn as father and son. Everyone in the family knows the history of that plant and we often give out cuttings from it to relatives and friends, as a token of love and longevity. All the cuttings, or 'slips' as we sometimes call them, have grown into beautiful, big plants which I like to believe represent the continued unity and strength within our family.

Derek, Glenn and I led an outwardly happy life together but Cooke's legacy still haunted me. It was a bit like having a row of boxes inside my head. Every now and again something would nudge one of the boxes and open it a crack. Negative emotions would seep out and threaten my happiness and stability.

After a while it would be forced shut again and everything would be fine until something else came along and knocked the lid off the next box in the line. It was a cycle I couldn't break out of, but it was manageable as long as good things kept happening and I could stay on a level course.

Derek transferred from the Navy into the Air Corps and we had our first child together. We had another boy called Cian* and were ecstatic about the new addition to the family. With our growing family, we needed a bigger home and so, in the early-1990s, we moved to a three-bedroomed house in the Tallaght area of Dublin. The house was lovely and spacious and was in a private cul-de-sac. Life should have been perfect for us, but the unresolved trauma in my childhood was always lurking in the background, as if waiting for a chance to resurface. That line of boxes was always liable to pop a lid and threaten my hard-won contentment.

As much as I loved the new house, I felt quite isolated there when Derek was away. It was a fair distance from my family and so I was on my own with the kids a lot of the time. Being alone and watching my sons grow up meant I had too much time to dwell on events from my own troubled childhood and so I tried to put thoughts out of my head by making new friends. When I could get a baby-sitter I would go to Bingo or the pub and became very good at pretending everything was okay, even when inside I felt like I was dying.

I was out shopping with a friend one day when all the boxes in my head were suddenly shaken simultaneously ajar as I stood frozen in shock. In the distance I had spotted Eamonn Cooke, shuffling along without a care in the world. He looked exactly the same, only older, and I was instantly

* : name changed.

overcome with fear. My friend saw that something was wrong but I could barely answer her when she asked me what had happened. All I could mutter between shallow panic-stricken gulps for breath was, 'I have just seen a nightmare from my past – I have to get out of here.'

Later that evening, I told Derek I had seen Cooke and he asked me if I was sure. There wasn't a single doubt in my mind because I could never forget that man if I tried. I remember sitting on the end of my son's bed, just watching him as he slept, and then the full horror of what Cooke had done to me hit me like a steam train. I saw how small and innocent my own children were. I was like that once – until Cooke had got his hands on me. In that moment, the boxes in my head shattered into tiny pieces and I knew then that no matter how I tried I'd never be able to stick them together again.

Shortly after seeing Cooke in the shopping centre, I started having horrific nightmares. In one of my most vivid dreams, I was living back in my old flat but it was on the ground floor. I was outside the building and saw that all the windows were barred. I was locked out and, hard as I tried, I couldn't get inside. As I peered through the window, I saw Cooke inside, lifting up my youngest son and taking him into the bedroom. My baby was screaming and crying for me but I couldn't reach him.

When I woke up I was dripping with sweat and my throat was dry. I was sobbing and screaming and Derek woke up with a start. He got a terrible fright when he saw the state I was in. I explained my nightmare to him and he held me and tried to comfort me, but I was still in a blind panic. I resisted his embrace and got up as my first instinct was to check on the children, even though I knew any danger was purely in my mind.

I tried really hard to put these thoughts out of my head but the dreams kept coming. Night after night they repeated themselves, like a broken record. One evening I went out for a few drinks with a friend and confided in her about how Cooke had hurt me. That night I slept through undisturbed until morning and cottoned on to the fact that if I had a few drinks on me, I didn't get the nightmares. I knew it wasn't the answer to my problems, but I grasped at it as if it was my only lifeline. It was a coping mechanism I latched on to to help me get to sleep. If I didn't have a drink, the nightmares returned with a vengeance. The dreams started to vary, but they always had the same theme; I was locked outside a building while Cooke had my children inside. The weather was always bright and sunny outside but inside it was cold and dark.

I started to question everything. I would see how vulnerable and small my children were and inevitably I asked myself how I would react if anyone hurt them. For the first time, I questioned if my parents had done the right thing when they discovered that Cooke had abused me. I also began to feel uncontrollably angry. Being a parent had changed the way I looked at everything, and not being able to cope with this new perspective, I began to drink more and more. I drank when I got angry. I drank when I became fearful. I drank to fend off the nightmares. Slowly I fell into a pattern of using drink to block out the suppressed horrors that were emerging from my past life. I couldn't cope with the shocking reality of a childhood that suddenly seemed Technicolor clear to me. It was no longer an unpleasant memory I could hide, it was a vivid and overwhelming nightmare from which I couldn't wake up.

I didn't drink every day but I would use alcohol several times a week to lessen my darkest moments. I saw it as a means of escaping the traumas that plagued me on a daily basis. They were still there when I put the bottle down, but when I felt the alcohol numbing my senses, it was like having a little holiday from the chaos raging inside my head. Booze acted like a dimmer switch, turning down the blinding spotlight that shone so cruelly and relentlessly on the past I'd tried desperately to forget.

I also started to experience flashbacks for the first time. Incidents that I had blocked out since childhood came flooding back to me as vividly as if they had happened the day before. One concerned a strange incident involving Cooke. I was just a little girl and he was still abusing me then. I remember waking one night and wanting to go to the toilet, which was downstairs in our house. I looked out of the window and saw Eamonn Cooke at the top of a telegraph pole at the bottom of our garden. The pole overlooked my bedroom window. I had no idea what he was doing up there. In fact, he was probably working on the telecommunications for his radio station, but I thought he had climbed up there just to watch me. I also thought that was how he knew what was going on in my life and how he could read my mind. I was so frightened to leave my room, in case he saw me, that I went for a wee in the corner of my bedroom.

It was only a flashback, but I realised I must have been far more afraid of Cooke than I had ever admitted to myself at the time. I had always believed I wasn't scared, but now my sub-conscious was telling me another story. When I saw Cooke that time in the hospital, I had no children of my own. I often wonder how I would have reacted if they had already been born then. If I'd have chosen to leave him there, in the peace he didn't deserve.

I went to a social function with my parents and they noticed I was drinking far more heavily than I had done before. I knew I was abusing alcohol but still tried to convince myself I was only drinking to help me sleep. That evening I stayed at my parents' house and, to my great shame, I lost control and went absolutely ballistic at them. What I didn't say to them is nobody's business. Drunk and out of control, I lost the plot and starting screaming obscenities in their faces.

'Jaysus Christ, why didn't you do something, for fuck's sake?' I screamed at Daddy. 'I would cut the balls off anyone who did that to my kids. I would do life for them. Why didn't you just batter him or hurt him in some way? That was my life he destroyed.'

Mammy also bore the brunt of my anger.

'Why weren't you watching me – what were you doing while Eamonn Cooke was abusing me?' I raged at her.

While giving vent to my anger, I didn't stop to consider that I had grown up in very different times, when parents genuinely believed it was safe for children to play out in their own neighbourhoods. I was just lashing out at the people closest to me without a thought for what they'd been through too. I had lost sight of the fact that the only person who had ever abused or hurt me was Eamonn Cooke.

Violent and ugly in my drunken temper, I was blaming my parents for the misery that still haunted me from those dark childhood days in Inchicore. I was hurt, and at that moment didn't care that I was also hurting my parents. I was transferring my pain on to them – a clear example of how the ripple effect works in child abuse. It is never just one person who is damaged by a pervert like Cooke, whole families can be destroyed by the devastation of abuse. Until that point in my life, I didn't know it was possible to experience such rage, All these pent-up feelings were pouring out of me like something out of *The Exorcist*.

'I did the best that I could at the time,' Mammy tried to explain. I now know that was the truth, but in my rage I couldn't be reasoned with. Instead, I taunted her by saying she never knew exactly what he had done to me. I had no intention of ever telling her or Daddy; I was just trying to push their buttons and get a reaction. It didn't occur to me that my family couldn't help me with something I had chosen never to confide in them before.

I also told Mammy that I had spoken to a friend about the abuse I'd suffered at Cooke's hands.

'Why have you started to talk about this now?' she asked.

'If I want to talk about it, I will. Just because *you* can't face up to it doesn't mean I can't. It's my life we are talking about here,' I said aggressively.

Mammy said it wasn't because she didn't want to talk about it, it was just that she found it very upsetting and distressing. She hadn't been prepared for my temper or my vicious outburst. The following day she tried to talk to me when I was sober, but very little she said sank in.

Mammy and Daddy were extremely concerned at the changes they witnessed in me. They say the truth comes out in drink, but in my case I think it was more confusion and that I was just using my drinking as a mechanism to cope with my past life. They asked me to seek help because they knew something was terribly wrong, but they didn't know how to help me themselves. They told me they had never seen me like that before and that they hadn't recognised their own daughter in such a drink-fuelled rage.

I returned home to Derek and the kids but remained unsettled and bad-tempered. Derek couldn't say a word to me without me taking his head off. I was impossible to live with but, unfortunately, this was only the beginning of a pattern that would last for some time. Now my fury was unleashed there was no turning back. I didn't row with my family all the time, but every time I went out with my parents for a social evening, it always ended the same way. My anger fuelled by the demon drink, there seemed to be no stopping me. I let rip at Mammy and Daddy because they couldn't tell me what I wanted to hear. They couldn't turn the clock back either or reverse the hurt that Cooke had caused me. There was little they could say to console me when I lost control of my temper.

The next day Mammy would always try to talk to me, but it must have been very hard for her, especially with her daughter continually throwing the blame on her. I always apologised the next day, when I had sobered up, but I had already inflicted terrible hurt on my parents by then. They suffered hours of me rambling on like a broken record about something none of us could change. We were still all as helpless as we had been all those years ago when Father Nolan had dropped the bombshell of truth on my parents.

Life continued in the same vein for some time. I continued to struggle with the memories and damage of Cooke's abuse, and I continued to abuse alcohol whenever it became too much for me. On one of the worst occasions I suffered hallucinations. One night I believed I saw two men in the house and took a cricket bat and swung it at them. Glass shattered all around me as the bat crashed through the windows, but there were no men standing there at all. They were merely figments of my booze-fuelled imagination.

I drank consistently throughout my twenties to numb the pain of my past, but I still had a young family and a home to run so my drinking never completely took over my life. My sons remained my anchor, preventing my life from running completely adrift, but Derek knew I was in trouble and would say, 'You can't go on like this, you have to get yourself sorted. I can't be with you all the time. I have to go out and earn a living, to look after our family.' He was right, of course, but I just played the victim and accused him of not understanding.

The truth was I barely understood what was happening to me. Just like my parents, Derek did not know the full extent of Cooke's abuse of me because I was too ashamed to tell him. Added to this was the constant feeling of anxiety. I couldn't bring myself to trust anyone outside the family around my kids. I was always watching the boys for signs that something might be wrong. They were allowed to play outside but only when I could see them, and I refused to let them go to sleepovers at friends' houses. I would sometimes watch them playing innocently in the park, laughing on the swings or running around shouting, and would be both terrified for their innocence and filled with sadness at what had happened to mine.

Friends I confided in were horrified when I told them what had happened. They always asked, 'How did you get through that? What help were you given?' Until very recently I had believed that I'd never needed any help. I didn't understand that you could experience a delayed reaction to traumatic events. My emotions of fear and sorrow had always been there. I had just suppressed them in a bid to deny they existed because it was the only way I felt I could survive.

One day Derek came home and said he had finally had enough. He had returned from work to find me once again at a friend's house talking while the children were with a baby-sitter at home. He told me I had to get a grip on myself. It was tough love but he was right. I knew I was out of control emotionally, but I didn't know how to rescue myself. My anger was all but destroying me and it seemed to be worse when I looked at my growing children, their innocence and fragility. I was eaten up with rage and knew it was going to overwhelm me. I thought about how I wanted to castrate Cooke and hurt him for all the bad things he had inflicted on me. I was also convinced that someone wanted to hurt my children and imagined countless scenarios where I would be helpless to protect them. It was like a conscious extension of my nightmares. If family or friends gave my sons an innocent hug, I was filled with apprehension and terror. I was constantly looking for clues to see if they were the victims of abuse too. My entire life was filled with fear and misery.

Derek had shown the patience of a saint. He put up with me because he knew I had lost my way, but at the same time he was no fool and wasn't prepared just to let me throw my life away. More importantly, it was our family as a whole he was thinking about. Our lives were in crisis because of my emotional state. I smoked heavily and lived on my nerves. It was only a matter of time before the whole pack of cards caved in. I wanted to do right by Derek and the boys so I tried to help myself by getting involved at the children's schools. I joined the Parent Teacher Association, just to have something different to focus on instead of the thoughts endlessly circling in my head.

I stopped drinking so much and when I cut back my anger subsided too. I began to talk to Mammy and Daddy properly, instead of just shouting at them in a drunken fit. I told them I was truly sorry for all the terrible things I had said to them and the hurt I had put them through. I felt so guilty now that I had partly blamed them for crimes that were all Cooke's. All Mammy and Daddy had ever done was love me.

In 1996, Derek and I were blessed with the birth of our third son, Ryan*. I lived for Derek and the boys and they brought me so much joy, but still I couldn't shake off the trauma of my childhood abuse. All I had ever wanted was to feel normal, to get on with my life as other people did. I wasn't ambitious and I didn't crave the high life; family had always been the most important thing to me. And mine was being poisoned by the wrong that had been done to me as a child.

* : name changed.

13

Around the time I was starting to make amends and gradually deal with my problems without relying on the crutch of a few drinks, I accidentally came across a newspaper article that had been published a year earlier. I had bought a new handbag and it had been stuffed with newspaper to help keep its shape. When I pulled the paper out, a photograph caught my eye. I unscrewed the newsprint and there was Cooke's twisted face staring back at me. As I started to read the article, I was stunned by what I discovered. Cooke had been campaigning against the Catholic Church on behalf of his latest wife Jane who said she had been raped and abused by a priest when she was a young child.

When I got to the end of the article, I felt physically sick. There, in black and white, was Eamonn Cooke campaigning for the rights of abused children when he was an abuser himself! How he had the nerve to go on record attacking paedophiles in the Church when he himself had spent more than twenty years abusing kids was beyond me. He was now one of Ireland's best-known radio personalities and was using his position to castigate the clergy for taking away a child's innocence. This, the very same man who had robbed me of mine. He'd abused so many children over the years and yet he still had the audacity to put his name to this cause and his face in the paper, for all his victims to see. He really must have believed he was beyond the law. Like me, his victims had obviously been too frightened to come forward.

Jane had married Cooke in 1989 in a Blackpool register office. She was twenty-three at the time and looked a lot younger. At fifty-two, he was more than twice her age.

In 2003, after Cooke was sentenced for a long list of child sex abuse charges against myself and other children, Jane Cooke spoke publicly about the way her husband helped her campaign against the Church. She said she'd had no idea he was a paedophile and that it sickened her how, of all people, it had been in him she'd confided about a childhood incident when she had been raped and abused by a priest. Jane claims it wasn't until her husband was convicted that she realised he too was a paedophile. Little wonder, perhaps, that he was the first person ever to believe her story. After all, he was no stranger to paedophilia himself.

Jane Cooke told Ireland's *Evening Herald*, 'When I found out about him, it was the greatest kick in the teeth I ever got; to think of him doing that while supporting my case. He must have been getting his jollies when I was telling him about the abuse I went through. He has ruined my life and the lives of those kids he abused. When he was helping with my case against the Church he was nearly crying in front of me when the abuse was mentioned. It turns out he is the same.'

Before all this, though, back in 1995, Jane Cooke was one of the first victims to go public on Ireland's clerical abuse, with Cooke at her side championing her cause. She said she was sexually abused by a Catholic priest in 1976 when she was just ten years old. Like Cooke with his victims, she said the priest gave her sweets and loose change. In June of 1995, Cooke told newspapers that had the Church admitted responsibility and responded with an apology when the abuse took place, he and his wife would not be protesting. They were planning on taking their case to the Vatican and were raising funds for the trip. He then arranged a press conference for Jane at the Lansdowne Hotel in Dublin where she told reporters that her husband had taped conversations with the priest in question and sent them to the Archbishop's house.

The whole scenario had sickening parallels with Cooke's own abuse of me and his other victims. When I read that article it completely tipped me over the edge. I tore around the house like a woman possessed, before grabbing the article and running to a friend's house across the road.

'Look at that bastard,' I screamed. 'How dare he stand up in public and campaign against paedophiles when he is one of them?'

When my friend finally calmed me down, I decided to go and see a priest to tell him what had happened. I was beginning to think I was going mad. How could Cooke have got away with such audacity?

'Father, I need to talk to you about something,' I said. 'It's not a confessional but I am very upset about something that happened to me in my past. I have come to you because I want to do something about this man, but I am too frightened to go to the police. I have three young children and want to know if you can help me to get this man investigated.'

I then outlined my story and he listened to me intently. Afterwards he said he would speak to the Bishop to see how they could help.

My nightmares came back with a vengeance and as I had just had my third baby I was totally exhausted. It was hard enough raising three children, but waking up still reeling from the horrors of those dreams was pushing me to my limits.

Flashbacks from my time at Cooke's began to mingle with my nightmares, the past colliding with the present. I felt I was back in Cooke's house, but instead of me being in his bed it was my children. I could see Cooke's face but as hard as I tried to burst through the bedroom door, it wouldn't open. I had further visions of him bathing naked children in the bathroom, but couldn't make out the children's faces. I was so afraid I was losing the plot that I went to see my GP. It so happened she was one of the two doctors who had examined me as a child, after Cooke had abused me. I reminded her that my medical records should show I'd been abused by him and she said, 'Oh, yes, that's a long time ago.'

I explained about the newspaper article and confided that I believed he was still abusing children. I told her about my nightmares too. She said she understood my concerns but encouraged me to focus on my new baby and young family. She prescribed me some anti-depressants to help relieve my anxiety. I felt bereft when I left her surgery that day as I really didn't feel this was the answer I'd been looking for.

I was still very confused about why I'd never opened my mouth to tell anyone what was happening to me as a child. I was trying to fathom a child's innocence with a troubled adult mind, and the result was nothing but confusion for me. How *could* he have manipulated me into keeping silent? I failed to remember that I was just a child then, too intent still on blaming myself for his crimes.

The burning fury inside me refused to go away. I began constantly taking showers because I felt dirty and soiled. I scrubbed and scrubbed at my skin until it was red raw and painful. But no matter how long I stood under that shower, it wasn't long enough to wash away the feelings I had harboured for so many years. I was totally exhausted – mentally, physically and emotionally.

Several agonising months passed. I'd heard nothing from my local priest so I went back to visit him. I felt I had a duty to pursue the matter. He told me he had spoken with the Bishop who said that Cooke was a very dangerous man, but that I should leave well alone. It was at that moment that a light bulb went on in my head. Here I was, almost twenty years after Cooke abused me, talking to clergy and doctors – and they were telling me the very same thing they had told Mammy all those years ago! Nothing had changed. Now I found myself in the same helpless place that she had found herself back in 1978. I knew in my heart that Cooke hadn't changed his ways and that other children must be in danger. Who was going to speak up for them? The thought nearly killed me.

I suffered my worst ever nightmare the night after I'd spoken to the priest. It started like the others, with me locked outside of a house, but on this occasion I was able to get inside. The house was dark and derelict and there were dozens of children everywhere, children I had never seen before, crawling over the floor. Their faces were pale and haunted-looking, as if in a horror film, and as I tried to walk through the house they started grabbing at my legs, screaming for help. Their dull eyes turned up to mine, they were begging me to rescue them. I began to walk out of the house, saying there was nothing I could do, and woke then to the sound of my own screams.

From this whole turbulent period, I do at least retain one beautiful memory of a day when I was able to forget everything bad and have the time of my life. When Ryan was almost one, Derek and I finally decided to get married. It was a very special day that we shared with our children, our families and friends. Momentarily, my demons were forgotten and I was able to concentrate on my wedding to the man with whom I was deeply in love. It came at a very traumatic time in my life, but I was still able to enjoy the day. I remember feeling proud and happy to become Derek's wife. It was also a day filled with laughter and some highly amusing unforeseen hitches!

The day began when I discovered that our Jack Russell dog had sneaked into the bathroom overnight and eaten all the flowers that had been stored in there to keep them cool. With just hours to the wedding, I had to race around trying to find buttonholes for the men and a bouquet for myself. Eventually, I found a flowerseller who was able to give me flowers for the men, but they looked more like bushes and I had to trim them back. We fell about laughing because it was like trying to pin miniature forests on to the men's jackets. I managed to salvage what I could of my bouquet and added in a few fresh flowers to replace the ones the dog had eaten. Luckily, none of the guests were any the wiser!

The service was beautiful and we were blessed to have a wonderful priest to marry us. He had everyone laughing when he told the congregation, 'Traditionally, newlywed couples go off on their honeymoon to get to know one another intimately. As you all know, Siobhan and Derek already have three children and so they will be going on their honeymoon for a rest and have asked if there are any volunteers for baby-sitters!' There was also a special blessing during the service when I narrowly averted disaster for the second time. Derek and I were supposed to light candles together, to show our unity, but when it was my turn I leaned over and singed the lace on my dress, burning my arm. It could have been far worse if I had gone up in flames on the altar and we still laugh about it today.

After the service, there was a military guard of honour for us and we went on to a fabulous reception in Derek's mess at the air base barracks. He had also organised a special treat for me that day. A helicopter flew over the mess and a winch-man dropped down and delivered me a bottle of champagne and a box of chocolates, just like the Milk Tray television adverts. It was such a thrill, I couldn't wipe the smile from my face. There were lots of speeches and photographs with family and loved ones. I think Derek would have been happy enough to slope off to the Caribbean and get married on a beach, but I wouldn't have wanted it any other way than to be surrounded by our families. It was a traditional wedding and lots of people got quite drunk, especially as beer was very cheap in the mess. I think it was the first time I saw someone falling up a set of stairs instead of down!

We went to the Canary Islands for our honeymoon and it was bliss. I felt calm and at peace, temporarily released from the hidden traumas that were the legacy of Eamonn Cooke.

When we returned home, I tried to maintain that feeling of peace and be as normal as possible, looking after my family with a smile on my face, but the turmoil inside resumed and intensified. I began doing voluntary work to shift my thoughts away from Cooke but, no matter what I did, every night the horrors came alive again as I tried to go to sleep. Some nights, I would see the faces of the other children he'd abused. There was one dream where I was an adult, walking in Phoenix Park with a friend; we were two young mothers out with our children, enjoying the sunshine and the flowers. When we went to leave, we couldn't find our children. My heart flipped over and we ran around the park, trying to find them, calling their names. I turned to face the road and saw Cooke driving off in his Jaguar car, with all the children crammed in the back seats. Their faces were pressed against the windows and they were banging on the glass, screaming out to their mammies for help. Once again, there was nothing I could do and I woke to the sound of my children's imaginary screams still ringing in my head.

As sleep brought me nothing but these horrors, I began to stay awake at night. I would often find myself up at four in the morning, cleaning the house and then scrubbing myself over and over. I could hardly eat and I chain-smoked. Then one day I stood in the kitchen, peeling potatoes, and without thinking about it, I just took the potato knife and sliced it into my hand. Momentarily, I felt the tension drain away from me, as I watched the blood drip into the sink. I can't explain why I did it; I knew I just had to hurt myself to take my mind off all the feelings of anger and fear. My family was worried sick about me, but I don't think even they realised the extent of my mental disintegration.

I ached, body and soul. I'd reached a point of desperation when all I wanted was to go to sleep and never wake up. In my mixed-up mind, I truly believed that my family would be better off if I never woke up. I thought I was the one creating the problems, and because I couldn't fix myself then everything was my fault. I adored my family but thought I would do the right thing and remove my misery from their lives. When I went to bed after deciding this, I felt calmer than I had in years. I didn't specifically think that I was going to kill myself – that didn't even enter my head. I just knew that if I went to sleep, I would be rid of everything. I got into bed and kissed Derek goodnight.

'I'm going to sleep now,' I said.

Derek turned over and I waited a while until I was sure he had dropped off, then I swallowed a handful of very strong tablets that had been prescribed for me by the doctor to combat my anxiety and depression. I washed them down with gulps of water and slowly drifted into unconsciousness. I don't remember precisely how many tablets I took but I do know it was enough to numb the pain and put me out cold. My plan had worked. The tablets had put me to sleep. The next thing I knew, I was in hospital, surrounded by doctors and nurses pumping my stomach. I looked up and saw Derek's anxious face and just thought, *Oh, fuck, now I've got some explaining to do.*

My husband had called an ambulance, fearing I was dead, when he'd realised I had swallowed some pills and he couldn't rouse me from sleep. He had tried to wake me but panicked when I didn't respond.

Medics at the hospital made me drink some foul-tasting charcoal-type drink, to force me to regurgitate the contents of my stomach. When I came round, a doctor came to see me and asked why I had taken the tablets. I told him I had been abused as a child and was struggling to cope with the memories. He said he was unable to deal with such issues but recommended I seek counselling and help from a psychiatrist. I remained in hospital for two days before returning home. The whole episode is a bit of a blur but I do remember everyone asking me how I could be so selfish when I had young children at home. I didn't know how to answer them because I didn't know how to explain the way I felt inside. I was desperate and believed I couldn't talk to anyone, not even Derek, because I had been enough of a burden on him already. The episode left me feeling isolated and filled with shame.

I took the overdose just three months after I married and feel terrible guilt about it today. I can't imagine how Derek must have felt when his wife did such a thing, so soon after our beautiful wedding and honeymoon. I can't explain it myself, except by saying I just couldn't cope with my feelings any longer and simply wanted to escape from them. I didn't recognise that I was unwell at the time.

I decided to take the advice of the hospital doctor and seek professional help. I went to see a psychiatrist in September 1997, but as soon as I mentioned child sex abuse he said he was not able to deal with my case. He prescribed me the controversial anti-depressant Seroxat and referred me instead to a counselling service known as LARAGH. I went home and threw the pills in the bottom of the drawer, knowing that the answer to my problems didn't lie in medication. I had already tried a course of anti-depressants and was not confident that they worked; I couldn't see why this prescription would be any different. But I was prepared to try the counselling service.

LARAGH was established in 1993 by the Eastern Regional Health Authority in response to the huge increase in demand for counselling services relating to child sex abuse. In the early-90s child sex abuse in Ireland attracted unprecedented media attention, in particular when the true scale of abuse by members of the clergy began to become known. This prompted many more victims to come forward and confide about their own childhood traumas.

I will never forget my first and only appointment with LARAGH. It was in October, a month after I had visited the psychiatrist, and I arrived on time, feeling nervous but hopeful that someone would finally be able to help me get my life back on track. My hopes would prove to be short-lived.

I was introduced to a counsellor who asked me a series of questions, including the name of my abuser. When I refused to give up Cooke's name, she told me that LARAGH was unable to help me unless I was prepared to identify the perpetrator of the sex crimes against me and go to the Garda. I was still too fearful of Cooke to put his name out there in public. Even the Bishop of Dublin and my GP had warned me off such a course and told me that Cooke was a dangerous man whom I should leave well alone. The petrol bombing of one of his other victims served as a significant example of the risks involved in confronting or opposing him. And now here was this counsellor, a complete stranger, asking me to name him before LARAGH would agree to counsel me.

I left the clinic that day and returned home after receiving absolutely no help or support from a service that had been set up specifically to deal with adult victims of child abuse. I don't think I have ever felt so alone in the world as I did at that time. I had asked for help and been refused. I don't believe that the system I encountered had any concept of the fear that abuse victims carry into their adult lives. It was an utter travesty that I was refused counselling because I was too afraid to name my abuser. It was also a reflection on how much the support services in Ireland still had to learn if ever they hoped to help child abuse victims resolve their problems.

I sat up alone that night and thought about whether I should name Cooke in return for counselling, but just kept looking out of the living-room window, imagining a brick or a petrol bomb being thrown through the glass. I knew I wasn't ready to take that step; it was too great a risk. My nightmares continued to fuel my fears, and my fears continued to perpetuate my nightmares. I was trapped in this constant turmoil. All I could do was try to convince myself there were no further steps I could take to expose Cooke or save any other children from him in the future. But in my heart I don't think I believed that. I felt terrible guilt towards these children I didn't even know; the ones I imagined he'd abused over the past twenty years of my not coming forward and naming him. But even this wasn't enough to give me the courage to push myself that one step further.

I knew that if I wanted to be happy with my family and make a success of my life, I would have to make some serious changes, and soon. Having been let down by so many people when I had asked for help, I realised I was the only person who could make a difference to my own life. With no support from the State, the clergy or the medical profession, I tried harder than I ever had to push Cooke from my mind. I still had a strong faith in God and prayed often for guidance and help. However, I felt estranged from the representatives of the Catholic Church. I had asked members of its clergy to take on Eamonn Cooke, and in refusing to do so I believed they failed in their moral and pastoral duty to care for me and all the other innocent children of Ireland. They would not stand up and be counted when it mattered most.

At the time the Catholic Church was coming under heavy fire on the subject of the paedophile priests in its ranks, and all I can assume is that they didn't need the likes of me announcing their association with lay paedophiles like Cooke as well. Little wonder also that they didn't want me going public about the same inept and damaging advice they had given Mammy and me, twenty years apart, to keep quiet about these heinous crimes. Shame on the Church for slamming the door shut in our faces! But I still wanted God in my life, despite my feelings about my religion, because I valued the difference between right and wrong, good and evil. Just because I no longer 'kissed the altar' every week at Mass, didn't mean that God was not by my side. I realised that He was far more merciful and loving than any religion created by mankind.

I felt personally abandoned by the Church and so I turned to my family, the only people who had consistently been there for me. I began to open up to Mammy and gradually we started to unravel the mess that was my life. Whenever something bothered me, I spoke to her about it instead of bottling up the harmful feelings that had festered in my soul for so long.

The turning point came in 1998. Derek had been a huge support to me throughout my problems and one day he asked me what I really wanted to do with my life. Together, we formed a plan to give me a fresh start. I stopped drinking heavily and worked hard to recover my health. I also decided to stop hiding from my problems. I joined an alcohol awareness programme and they referred me to a counsellor who helped me enormously. I also knew I wanted to go back to work and do something I really enjoyed. For that I needed to learn to drive so Derek booked me lessons and bought me a little car. I was on the road to recovery. We bought a caravan, too, so that we could get away with the boys and spend some much-needed family time together.

In June that year I approached a man who knew my father very well. He ran what was reckoned to be the biggest indoor market in Europe and I asked him if I could take a stall to sell Irish music there. I was thrilled when he agreed, pleased and proud to take my space in Windsor Market in Dublin and begin selling music. It was the start of a business which is still thriving today. I found that I had a knack for dealing with the public and enjoyed my work immensely. Even though I only worked on Sundays when the market was open, I looked forward to it every week and found a new source of enthusiasm in my life. Going back to work helped restore my sanity and get my life back on track.

Some time after I had been working at the market, though, and was at last feeling more positive about my future, my whole life was turned upside down yet again. I set off for Dublin one Sunday morning unaware that my world was about to change forever. My sister Adrienne was helping me that day and it started just like any other. I'd had a good morning, sold some tapes, and was about to get some lunch. I glanced up from the stall and through the bustling Sunday shoppers caught sight of the one face I'd hoped never to see again. Eamonn Cooke was strolling towards my stall with the arrogance of someone who had nothing to be ashamed of. As he came closer, I froze in sheer blind panic and felt my blood run cold. To my horror, he was clutching the hands of two little children. They must have been roughly the same age I'd been when he started abusing me. As I looked at them, I saw myself as a child. They were beautiful children but when I looked at them more closely I saw their expressions were blank and their eyes soulless. It was as if the life had been drained from them, and I knew in that instant that Cooke was abusing them.

I felt as if I was going to vomit there and then. I felt weak and my legs turned to jelly. I thought my heart was going to burst through my chest. I was frightened and sickened all at once, and truly believed my legs were going to buckle underneath me. Everything else in the market seemed to become a blur. I couldn't hear anything around me. It was as if I was free-falling in slow motion and all I could focus on were the faces of those little children. They looked like lambs to the slaughter. I was overwhelmed with dread and fear for them. My head was spinning. I felt almost paralysed as I looked on in helpless disbelief, the tears rolling down my cheeks.

'You look dreadful, what's wrong?' asked my sister who'd noticed my tears. I hadn't even realised I was crying.

'It's Cooke, the bastard!' was all I could manage to say.

Adrienne went as white as a sheet and stood rooted to the spot at her end of the stall, rigid with fright.

'Don't serve him, Siobhan, don't serve him,' she said. 'Tell him to get lost.'

'I can't do that,' I replied under my breath. 'I don't want him to know it's me.'

It was at this point that Adrienne noticed the two children with him. 'Oh God, Oh God, Oh God,' she whispered. 'He hasn't stopped . . . he hasn't stopped. Oh, Jaysus,' she repeated in disbelief. We were both devastated.

Cooke looked barely any different from how I remembered him when I was a child. He was older and seemed much smaller, but his pinched and wizened face and cold, dead eyes were unmistakable, even after twenty years. The dirty old pervert was still shuffling around in his filthy dark suit and I could see the dirt on the back of his collar. If he had moved closer I am sure I would have been able to smell the acrid reek of him, from decades of smoking and never washing. It had been one thing seeing his horrible face in the newspaper, but it was an altogether more terrifying experience to see him standing in close proximity to me.

I realised he was also with a woman who by now had selected a tape from my stall. It was by a famous Irish group called the Wolfe Tones and was their twenty-fifth anniversary double cassette. Cooke handed over a note to pay for it, placing it on my counter. I didn't know what to do. I couldn't tell if he'd recognised me and was barely suppressing an overwhelming desire to lash out at him. I didn't want to serve him, but if I made a scene I was afraid he would realise who I was. Anger churned inside me. Before I could stop myself, I'd snatched the money from my counter, spat on it, then thrown it to the ground. Cooke simply walked off without uttering a word.

As sure as night follows day, I was now certain that he was still abusing children. I was also certain I had to do something about it. I had to get Cooke locked away for good and vowed to myself I would do whatever it took.

14

That was my Road to Damascus moment – the defining point at which I knew my life could never be the same again. Seeing Cooke in the cold light of day with two young children whose eyes betrayed the sadness I still felt myself had left me with no choice: I had to summon the courage to fight back or else the mental torment that had resulted from his abuse of me would continue unchecked.

I told Derek I had seen Cooke because I knew that if I kept it bottled up inside it could destroy me. He was very concerned and cautious because he feared the sighting might act as a catalyst to send me spiralling out of control again. He watched me like an anxious parent, extremely worried that my self-destructive behaviour might start up again. I didn't sleep that night as the events of the last twenty-four years replayed themselves over and over in my mind. I had worked hard towards my recovery, trying to erase all memories of the abuse, but now my conscience was pulling me in the opposite direction. I had to help the children still in Cooke's grip. I didn't recognise the faces of those poor little mites I'd seen in the market, but I knew they were innocent and, like the children in my nightmares, needed to be rescued from that monster. I thought back to my childhood when Daddy told me about the Angel Guardian who sat on my shoulder to guide and protect me. I prayed that night for all the protection my angel could bestow on me.

For a while I wrestled with the dilemma facing me. I knew I had to do something, but still had no clear plan of how to move forward. Fate played a huge part in what happened next. I fell pregnant again and in June 1999 gave birth to our first daughter, Miriam.*

My market work had brought me into contact with a lot of people in the music industry and when I'd opened the stall, I'd met a woman called Joan Lawler who worked as a voluntary DJ for Radio Dublin. It might not have been as big as it was in its heyday, but Cooke's station was still on air. She would call by my store and buy music to play for her radio slot. As much as I hated Cooke, I was certain Joan had no idea of his wickedness and was always pleasant with her. She was a nice woman and I enjoyed talking with her but I was still heartbroken that music I supplied was being played on his radio station. She, of course, had no idea of who I was or of my connection with Cooke.

I hadn't seen her for a while when one Sunday Joan came to my stall to buy some music. She said that she was buying the tapes as presents because she no longer worked for Radio Dublin. We were idly gossiping together when she unwittingly threw a grenade into our conversation. She told me that the year before, in 1998, Cooke had been arrested for

* : name changed.

allegedly sexually abusing a young boy. My ears pricked up like never before as she continued to elaborate on her story. Cooke had, apparently, telephoned John Lennard, the radio station manager at the time, and asked him to bring some cigarettes to the police station where he was being questioned.

Joan went on to tell me of another incident that had taken place. Prior to his arrest, she'd heard that a Radio Dublin employee had walked into the station one day and found Cooke on the floor with two children resting their heads in his lap. Cooke was startled by the presence of the employee, as he had not been expecting anyone in the station at that time. Joan said the incident had left her feeling very uncomfortable. When her boss was later arrested, it compounded her feelings that something was not 'quite right', and both she and John packed in their jobs at the station.

Cooke then falsely claimed that John Lennard, whose real name off-air was Brendan Brophy, had tried to rip him off and had therefore been sacked from the radio station. He tried to make out that John was only looking to blacken his former boss's name because he'd been sacked by Cooke – a slur on a man who had acted entirely honourably.

History was repeating itself all over again. Twenty years after James Dillon had led the first exodus, further members of staff at Radio Dublin had walked out of the station after Cooke was accused of sexually molesting a child. Joan told me that Cooke was questioned at Ronanstown Police Station in Dublin and that a Detective Sergeant by the name of Gerry Kelly was involved in the investigation. I later learned that

Detective Inspector Todd O' Laughlin was heading the enquiry. He had previously worked on the infamous gangland murder of Irish journalist Veronica Guerin. When I heard he was involved, I knew the Garda had brought out some of their heavyweights and they obviously took the investigation very seriously.

I went home and discussed the news with Derek who said he would support me in whatever course of action I wanted to take. The following morning, I picked up the phone and asked to speak with Gerry Kelly. Fate had dealt me this hand and I believed the time was right for me to go to the police with all that I knew about Eamonn Cooke.

Naively, I believed I would be able to pass this information on to the police without having to become directly involved in criminal proceedings against him. I also hoped it might bring some closure to the trauma that had dogged my entire adult life. When I agreed to meet Gerry and his colleague Detective Garda Louise Tyrrell, it was almost the end of 1999. We were rapidly approaching the new Millennium. Little did I know that for me it would mark the start of a very long and painful trek down the road to justice.

I met the police in Bewleys Hotel at Newlands Cross in Clondalkin, on the outskirts of Dublin. Mammy and Daddy were with me. I told them that I had some information about a man called Eamonn Cooke whom I had heard they were investigating in relation to allegations of child abuse. I outlined my story and explained that I had not come forward before as I was frightened of Cooke, and because both Mammy and I had been advised to keep quiet by the Church and the medical profession. I didn't go into any great detail about the extent of the sexual abuse I'd suffered because I was far too embarrassed and ashamed to divulge such intimate information to people I had never met before. I did, however, beg them to keep investigating Cooke because I knew that he had been abusing children for many years. But I felt I'd barely given them anything. After all, what evidence did I have other than my own word? Gerry later told me I had in fact given him far more information than he had expected from a first meeting.

They asked all about my childhood: where I had lived and who my friends had been. They then asked me for a brief account of what had happened with Cooke, and even though it had happened a quarter of a century before I rattled off the details as though it had been yesterday. I gave them the names of some of the other children who'd visited the house with me. I also said Cooke had taken us children into his bed and touched us, and that we had seen him naked. I felt frightened and humiliated while giving this account because I had no trust in authority at that time. This would change over the years I worked with Gerry and his brilliant team of detectives to put Cooke away. At the end of our meeting they thanked me and said they would be in touch if they needed me again.

Christmas came and went and the new Millennium arrived full force. The year 2000 was to herald the beginning of a long and turbulent period in my life.

In January 2000 Gerry Kelly telephoned me to say that a woman who had been abused by Cooke as a child at the same time as me had made a full statement about his crimes. She was also prepared to go to court and give evidence if the police could make a case against him. The Garda asked if I would meet them again, and I agreed. We discussed the possibility of me making a statement against Cooke in relation to his abuse. They said they were not putting any pressure on me, it was just something for me to think about. I should contact them if I wanted to go ahead. I was genuinely shocked as this was not at all what I had expected.

Aside from the unpleasantness of seeing Cooke again and having to confront so many of my worst memories, my life was in a very good place by this time. I felt safe and happier than I had in a long while. My children were healthy and content, and Derek and I had never been so close. All of a sudden, I was faced with a huge decision: should I disrupt all this to pursue Cooke to justice?

I knew I had to think long and hard about my decision because, one way or another, it would affect the rest of my life. I had finally begun to believe that I had done nothing wrong and therefore didn't need to feel ashamed over what had happened to me as a child. But I was still scared to make a statement because if it became public knowledge that I had been abused, I was worried people might point and stare at me in the street. I had been demonised once before as a child and was terrified it might happen again. I didn't realise that my perceptions were warped because I had taken the guilt for Cooke's actions on myself for so long. I was also worried that my children might suffer by association if it became known that I was involved in a child abuse case. Would neighbours whisper in huddles and remember the scandal that had befallen us so long ago? Would they say there was no smoke without fire? I think I was scared of being punished all over again if people failed to understand that I was the victim here, my only 'crime' to have been a child who had fallen into the clutches of an abuser.

Derek and I talked and talked for what seemed like an eternity. Even though I carefully weighed up all the implications of taking Cooke to court, in my heart I believe my mind was made up from the very beginning. How could I stay silent when finally I had the chance to speak up? The image of those children in the market still haunted me. I had to go forward: for their sakes, for my sake, for my family's sake. I was scared witless of what was to come but confident that my children and family would support me throughout and never question my decision. If they were not proud of me for what I was about to do, then they wouldn't be the family I knew and loved.

This proved to be a crucial point in my marriage to Derek. I decided that if I was to go to court and testify against Cooke, it was something we had to do together. I had to consider his feelings, too, as he has always been a very private man. Derek backed me one hundred percent, not just because he was supporting his wife but also because he believed Cooke was a dangerous predator on young children and a very real threat to society. My husband's strong sense of morality gave him the strength to support me.

'Cooke is the kind of man who will always try to find a house for sale in a community full of kids. No one should have to live next-door to him. You are doing the right thing,' Derek said to me. That final reassurance was all I needed.

I picked up the phone and called Gerry Kelly to tell him I

would help in his case against Cooke. On Valentine's Day 2000 I went to Ronanstown Police Station and made a formal statement to Gerry and Louise.

I will never forget walking into that station. I was taken into a cold, square room with an old-fashioned wooden desk and chairs arranged around it. This was the place where I was supposed to open up my heart to complete strangers about some of the most intimate and horrifying parts of my life. These stark, forbidding surroundings made me feel very uncomfortable. All I could think was, *Is this really where I have to sit and tell them all the awful details about what that man did to me?*

But Gerry Kelly and Louise Tyrrell couldn't have been nicer to me. They were lovely people, treating me gently and with great respect. It didn't make the process any easier, though. I didn't blame them for the fact that I felt so uncomfortable; nor did I blame them for the antiquated surroundings in which we had to speak. They were just doing their job in the surroundings our State saw fit to provide. Gerry and Louise asked me questions about Cooke and I tried to answer them as well as I could, but I felt terrible. I was so embarrassed that first day, I just wanted the whole episode to be over. I didn't go into very much detail, only giving the police basic information about how, as a child, I'd gone into Cooke's house and been touched by him. I didn't convey how serious the abuse had been because I was so ashamed. I had no idea how important my information would be to his prosecution. As far as I was concerned, not even my husband or my parents knew the exact nature of Cooke's abuse of me, and so it was almost impossible for me to articulate it fully now. I even considered leaving out the details about him performing oral sex on me, because I felt so degraded by telling them. I realised, however, that these were serious offences and, no matter how bad I felt, I had to describe them. So I explained about the garage and phones, the garden and the Can-can we'd danced. I told them about the film Cooke had made of us children and how he'd showed it to us on a projector in his bedroom. I also told them how he'd taken me and another girl into his bed and abused us. They wrote it all down and that interview formed the basic outline of my statement.

I think many people automatically assume that women feel more comfortable talking to a female police officer about sex crimes committed against them. For me, it was the opposite. To my way of thinking, Louise Tyrrell shared the same female anatomy as me and for that reason would know just how horrendous Cooke's actions had been, which made the shame even harder to bear for me. I felt such embarrassment that they both knew what had happened to me, but speaking to the female officer was more of an ordeal.

I will always regret that I didn't tell them about the time I ate the banana then woke up in Cooke's bed to discover blood on the sheets. The embarrassment I felt was too overwhelming. I feared they would find my account ludicrous. It wasn't until the trial that I realised Cooke had done that to other girls as well.

I explained to the two officers that other children went into Cooke's house, too, but only spoke to them about the abuses I saw and experienced. I couldn't speak for anyone else.

I went home that day with no back up or support. There

was no offer of counselling or any sort of safety net, despite my baring my soul to strangers about the horrors I had experienced. I felt totally rudderless, cast adrift in a very lonely sea, but was resolute that I wanted Cooke brought to justice. The public needed to know the truth about this sick bastard, most of all so that he would be prevented from abusing any other children. I never had any doubt in my mind that Cooke had continued his abuse of minors after I had passed out of his clutches. He had remained free to prey on the most innocent and vulnerable members of society for most of his adult life and was a master at grooming his victims, as I knew to my cost.

I was also aware that he must have changed the way he targeted his victims as public awareness of paedophilia grew. When I was a child, Cooke had the rich pickings of all the children in his immediate neighbourhood because their families were almost completely innocent of the very existence of it. In the 1990s he would have known he could no longer get away with behaving so flagrantly because of the keen media scrutiny and public outcry against perverts like him. He would have had to select and abuse his victims far more carefully if he wanted to continue evading detection.

The Internet is a wonderful tool of our modern world, but the downside of it is that it can also be used as a pervert's paradise. Where once kids were lured into paedophiles' homes with sweets, toys and puppy dogs, now they groom and trap naive victims online before arranging to meet their unsuspecting targets, who believe they've made new young friends in chat rooms. There is also a huge rise in the number of reports on the sex trade in foreign children. The media has highlighted the way children have been brought to places like Ireland and Britain for the express purpose of being supplied to sexual perverts. What happens to these children after they have been used and discarded by child molesters? Many go missing, and I shudder to think about their possible fate.

Ireland woke up to the scandal of paedophilia in the 1990s after Colm O'Gorman admitted in a current affairs documentary that he had been raped by a Catholic priest at the age of fourteen. The investigation, revealed in a BBC documentary called 'Suing The Pope', focused on Colm's torment after he was sexually abused by Father Sean Fortune, a parish priest in County Wexford. Father Fortune assaulted and raped his victim over a period of two and a half years. A BBC report in 2003 recounted the scandal as follows:

> The Bishop of Ferns, Dr Comiskey, admitted knowing there were allegations of child abuse surrounding a number of priests in his diocese when he was first appointed in 1984. But over the following fifteen years he failed to stop one of Ireland's worst clerical abusers, Father Sean Fortune, conducting a campaign of terror across his parishes. Bishop Comiskey refused to be interviewed, so he was confronted as he arrived to say Mass at his church in Wexford. He emerged from his car singing: 'We will survive' and immediately rebuffed the interviewer. Irish State broadcaster RTE re-screened Colm's film after massive public demand. Bishop Comiskey made

his resignation speech on the steps of his Wexford Palace the day before the broadcast. In his speech he said: 'My continuation in office could be an obstacle to healing . . . so I have tendered my resignation to Pope John Paul.' In fact Bishop Comiskey was effectively forced to resign. The Pope accepted his resignation. Father Fortune, the priest at the centre of the controversy, had been removed from one parish, only to be given another. He continued to be a disgrace, so Bishop Comiskey sent him to London to see a psychiatrist and to undertake a media course. He returned to Ireland and was made the director of a Catholic broadcasting and media training company. This gave him unlimited access to yet more boys.

Father Fortune was finally arrested in 1995 and charged with sixty-six counts of indecent assault and buggery. He committed suicide in the first week of his trial in 1999. Bishop Comiskey then fled his diocese, instead of reaching out to Fortune's many victims.

In 'Suing the Pope – the update', Colm O'Gorman tells how he tried to force the Church to admit the extent of its knowledge and cover-up of Fortune's record of abuse. The Irish Government then launched an inquiry and the country has since undergone something of a constitutional crisis. For the first time, the State has been forced to challenge the Catholic Church's authority and assert its dominance in law. Canon Law, which internally governs the Catholic Church, has been ridiculed by the Irish Minister for Justice who described it as being 'little more relevant than the rules of a golf club'. He warned the Church it could no longer use it as an excuse for withholding evidence. The Church has now abandoned its own 'independent audit' of child sexual abuse. However, Colm O'Gorman is still suing Bishop Comiskey, the Papal Nuncio and the Pope. They are still claiming diplomatic immunity from having to answer any questions about his rape by Father Fortune. For his courage in the face of his torment, Colm has received an 'Irish People of the Year' award by RTE.

O'Gorman's exposure of the Catholic Church sent the institution into virtual meltdown and prompted a huge surge of victims to come forward with similar horror stories about clerical abuse. Colm O'Gorman is also the founder and former director of One In Four, the national Irish charity that supports men and women who have experienced sexual abuse or violence. His bravery and courage in exposing the Church forced people to sit up and take notice. For the first time the public started to talk about this traditionally taboo subject. It was debated on television and radio, and many people were horrified to hear the details of what had gone on in their own country for decades. There were, though, a minority who still clung to the notion of an infallible Church, and a few diehards even attacked Colm for daring to speak out against their religion. He received hate mail asking,

'How dare you say such things about the clergy and the priests?'

Until this point, no one in our country had challenged the Church, which had remained untouchable and immune from criticism. Irish society's previous unwillingness to question the word from the pulpit made the country a perfect haven for paedophiles. It was against this backdrop that we went after Eamonn Cooke, five years after Colm O'Gorman's groundbreaking revelations. It was the right time to come forward.

Cooke was first arrested on allegations of child abuse in 1998 in relation to serious offences against a young boy, the same child Joan Lawler had mentioned to me. Then, in February 2000, he was arrested again in relation to a girl I had never met who had accused him of unlawful carnal knowledge, the legal term in Ireland for statutory rape. During the police interview, he was further questioned about abusing four other girls, including myself, during the 1970s. A few months later, and by pure coincidence, two sisters came forward to allege Cooke had abused them in the 1980s. He was arrested and questioned about their allegations in May 2000.

On 14 July that same year he was charged with twelve counts of buggery relating to a young boy, forty-four counts of indecent assault on five girls, sixteen counts of unlawful carnal knowledge of one girl, and one further attempted unlawful carnal knowledge on a separate child – a total of seventy-three charges in all. He also appeared in court in October 2000 when a further fifty sex abuse charges were laid against him in relation to the sisters who had been abused in the 1980s. Cooke was facing a total of more than 120 child sex abuse charges.

There are many women I know of who didn't come forward to give evidence against Cooke. Some remained too scared of him; others were just too ashamed to speak publicly about horrendous events from their past. I have always understood their fears and have never judged their decision to remain silent. After all, I too once refused to go to the Garda with a friend and it took me over twenty years to find the strength to go through with my case against Cooke.

In an unrelated investigation, he was sentenced to four months in jail for breaching a previous court order. Apart from this short spell in prison, Cooke remained on bail throughout the police investigation of him on the child sex abuse claims and I tried to continue with my own life as normally as possible, despite the prospect of the impending trial casting its shadow over my entire family. It was not easy, especially when I became the target of attempted intimidation by Cooke.

His criminal trial was due to start at the Four Courts in Dublin on 21 October 2002. By this stage, we had lost two of the original line-up of witnesses. A boy Cooke was accused of abusing withdrew his statement, saying he had made the story up, and one of the women also dropped out, terribly distressed and unable to face the ordeal ahead of her. That left six women, two of whom I knew and a further three I had not met before.

I was extremely nervous when I arrived at court and received my first introduction to the other victims. Gerry, who had by now been promoted to Detective Inspector, was also at the court with his team. As soon as we got there we were told we had to have an urgent meeting with the barristers and legal team who would be representing the State. Cooke's victims were all classed as State witnesses, we were told, and, as such, were not entitled to any legal representation. I didn't really understand the significance of that.

The State legal team then informed us that there would be a delay to the start of the trial. Cooke and his defence team were trying to argue that it shouldn't be allowed to go ahead because we had left it too long before coming forward with our allegations. The State countered Cooke's tactics by arguing that fear of our abuser had prevented us from speaking out earlier. The court subsequently ordered that the witnesses had to prove individually that each of us had suffered 'fear and domination' at Cooke's hands before being allowed to give evidence against him. This pre-trial would determine whether Cooke would in fact appear in court to face the charges made against him. In essence, we had to go through two procedures, so that not only was Cooke forcing his victims to relive their ordeals in front of him, he was making us do it twice.

The trial was immediately adjourned so that all the victims could be examined by clinical psychologists to assess our state of mind. These assessments would form a vital part of the pre-trial to determine whether Cooke would face a jury. It was the first of several examples of the delaying tactics which became the pattern of his defence over the ensuing years. He would do anything to slow down or disrupt the court process. It's my belief this was done in an attempt to grind down our resistance, but if anything it made me fight even harder.

I remember my interview with the psychologist clearly. He asked me a lot of questions about Cooke and how his treatment of me had affected my life. As far as I am aware, all the other women went through a similar process and the findings were eventually put before the court for a judgement. We also had to take the stand and swear to our evidence. The defence was bent on making things as hard as possible for all of us. We had to relate our individual experiences as Cooke sat there in the courtroom listening. It was a very daunting start to the trial because our validity as witnesses was being called into question even before the criminal proceedings had begun. Every one of us had our confidence dented by this process, as I am sure was the intention. Our former abuser was trying to break our spirit before the fight had really begun, but sadly for him he'd underestimated the strength of his opponents.

The pre-trial lasted into November and Cooke remained on bail throughout. Part of the conditions of this was that he was not to approach any of the witnesses in the proceedings. About a fortnight into the pre-trial I received a huge shock, however. By this stage I had moved from my stall into a shop unit in the market. I was standing there at work one Sunday when, out of the corner of my eye, I saw Cooke just a few yards away from me. He was holding the hand of a little blonde girl who at a guess must have been anything between the ages of eight and ten. She looked just like I did when I was her age. I panicked on the inside but told myself to keep calm.

Cooke looked at me and smiled. Then he bent down and

whispered something into the ear of the little girl. It was a sickening spectacle and he knew precisely the impact it would have on me. I realised he was trying to taunt me, this scarecrow figure from my nightmares, wearing the same smelly clothes. He knew I worked in the market, and bringing such a young girl before me in this deliberately provocative manner was sickening. It was as if he was saying, *No matter what you try and do to me, I'll still have children around me.* My first instinct was to lash out. Instead I walked over to a man I knew who ran a neighbouring stall.

'Excuse me, John,' I said. 'Can you please look and tell me, do you see a man standing over there, staring at me? I can't tell you what it's all about right now, but I will explain later.'

'I do,' he confirmed.

'Would you please, please, watch that man for me and keep an eye on the little girl too?' I asked, and John agreed.

He saw Cooke bend down and whisper to the child again. She walked past me and stopped at my shop unit, looked in, then walked out of another door.

Furious by now at this blatant attempt to reawaken bad memories for me, I rang the police and told them what had happened.

His actions that day demonstrated his supreme arrogance and complete disdain for the law. To procure a child and bring her in front of me in this way took some neck, when he was already on bail and not supposed to approach any of the witnesses in the forthcoming trial. Did he think I would still be too frightened to shop him to the Garda? Was he trying to play some perverted mind game with me, to see if he could get me to keep my mouth shut, the way I had as a child and for most of my adult life? He knew he had successfully managed to manipulate me all that time. It had to be worth another try. He'd shown no pity for me as a child, and even less to me as an adult by continuing to play his sick games in front of me.

I wasn't the only person he tried to intimidate either. Later, during the trial, he was spotted taking photographs outside the house of another witness. He seemed intent on tormenting us all.

When I spoke with the Gardaí, I asked them if they knew where Cooke was. They told me that he had failed to sign on with them that day in accordance with his bail conditions, and that they were searching for him. Eventually they found him in a car park near where I worked. It was not the first time the Gardaí had had to go looking for him either. On a previous occasion, he was found in a mobile home on a caravan park in Wexford. There were two children with him. Clearly this was a man with absolutely no fear of retribution. It seemed incredible to me that he'd ever been granted bail in the first place.

I don't know how I calmed myself enough to drive home that night. The next day I made a statement to the Garda which resulted in my having to attend yet another court hearing, to give evidence on his attempt to intimidate me. On 4 November 2002 I went to testify before a judge and Cooke was found to have broken his bail conditions. His bail was revoked and a warrant issued for his immediate arrest. He was picked up two days later on the Naas Road in Dublin and held in custody for the remainder of the trial.

My psychologist's assessment reported that I was suffering

from Post Traumatic Stress Disorder to a serious degree. In the opinion of the psychologist, I was still in genuine fear of Cooke and, therefore, I was allowed to proceed as a witness. It was the same for three of his other victims, but there was devastating news for the other two who had come forward. On the basis of their psychological reports, the court ruled they had failed to prove a fear of Cooke. Therefore, the charges he faced in relation to crimes committed against them were dropped and their cases thrown out of court. This was totally tragic and a scandal because both women were in fact severely traumatised by Cooke's actions and lived in misery and fear because of him. One of the women lost interest in everything she'd previously loved in life, following Cooke's abuse of her. She subsequently struggled to form any so-called 'normal relationships' and lived a reclusive life. She was very timid and, like I used to do, cleaned and washed herself obsessively. Her self-esteem was at rock bottom but, like many abuse victims, she had never fully acknowledged the extent of the damage inflicted on her by Cooke. This, was documented in the psychologist's report assessing her state of mind, and it proved enough to disqualify her from testifying against her abuser.

When I went in to meet my psychologist, I can clearly remember saying to him, 'I'm meeting you today because I have to meet you. I have never met you before, or been to see a psychologist before, and I don't really know what I'm here for. There is no way I can sit here and fully explain the impact Cooke has had on my life in just two or three hours. There are still some things I cannot speak about openly. And I don't think I ever will.'

I was aware the whole point of this procedure from the standpoint of the defence was to draw attention to the time that had elapsed since the alleged abuse. They were trying to say that it had taken too long for us to come forward with our statements, thereby undermining our status as reliable witnesses as well as potentially creating difficulties for the defence. The State was disputing this, arguing that our failure to come forward for so long was because we had spent most of our adult lives living in fear of Cooke, and were still dominated by memories of the abuse he had inflicted on us as children. But it was extremely hard to express that sense of fear and domination to a psychologist in the space of just a few hours. I know all the women felt this way, and it doesn't reflect on the professionalism of the psychologists who dealt with us. It was just the way the system worked – and for two of the women it clearly worked against them. We were asked to reveal the most intimate secrets of our lives to a person we had never met before and who knew nothing about us. As a result of this, two of Cooke's victims will never see justice served for the crimes he committed against them, and that is wrong.

It was very important to both those women that they should have their day in court. They had summoned up so much courage to come forward and finally give evidence against their abuser, and yet at the final hurdle were told that they could not. They were left feeling that they were not believed; that if Cooke were to serve any prison term it would not be for any of the crimes he had committed against them, which meant there would be no public record or acknowledgement of the abuses they'd suffered and the way their lives had been destroyed. For them, there was no justice on a personal level.

The two women were absolutely devastated by this outcome but they responded bravely and with dignity. Instead of running away, they sat with us every day in court as we proceeded with the trial. Not a day went by when they didn't turn up to support us. We really felt it was still the six of us against Cooke. Not once did the four witnesses who actually got to court see ourselves as any different from the two women who were not able to appear. We knew that we spoke for all six of us, and indeed all the many, many more women, known and unknown to us, who had suffered at the hands of Cooke.

It was very hard for them to be sidelined in a case which should have been about justice for them too. I have no doubt that those within the legal system believed Cooke was guilty of crimes against them but it was just the way our legal system worked and no one could do anything about it.

I think it is the first time that I opened my eyes to the flaws and peculiarities of the judicial system. In my mind, I always believed you went to court, you told the whole truth and nothing but the truth and, if you tell it as it is, then the bad man goes to prison, but I began to realise the reality of our legal system was nothing like that. This was a whole new challenge for me and it seemed like I was caught in a game of chess between two sides, pitting their wits against each other. All the little technicalities and loopholes were beyond my understanding at the time and I felt on very wobbly ground. I was worried every time

I opened my mouth in case I said the wrong thing, even if I was only telling my story honestly.

The decision that prevented them going to trial had a huge effect on their lives. As their cases were shelved, it meant that Cooke would not have to be tried on the charges specific to their allegations of abuse and neither of them could give evidence against him. One of the women had actually had a baby by Cooke when she was just a young teenager. I discovered in court that she was the girl I had seen all those years ago, getting out of Cooke's car shortly after he had stopped abusing me. She'd suffered terribly at his hands. It was the petrol bombing of her boyfriend's home for which he had been convicted in the mid-80s. Cooke was given a suspended four-year jail sentence for that. I'd had no idea, reading the report on that trial all those years before, that one day that woman and I would become fellow witnesses in search of justice against Cooke. It still seems very unfair to me that I was permitted to put my case against him and she was not.

I also began to query why the witnesses were not entitled to legal representation when the accused was. Eamonn Cooke was on Legal Aid, with some of the best barristers and lawyers in town retained to fight his corner, yet the people who had been hurt by him had no such help, no solicitors, not even an adviser to talk us through the complicated process of the law. Surely witnesses too should have the right to have legal procedure and jargon explained to them, every bit as much as the accused?

Back home I had a young family in need of my care, but it became apparent that for me normal life was very much on hold. It was like being in some kind of twilight zone where the ordinary routine of our lives had absolutely no importance. It was very, very hard for all of us to take.

15

We finally proceeded to trial on 18 November 2002. Senior Counsel Pat McCarthy and Isobel Kennedy led the prosecution for the State before Mr Justice John Quirke. Mr Blaise O'Carroll, Senior Counsel, defended Cooke. The only people who had no one to represent them were the witnesses, so we tried to support each other the best way we could. A lot of the procedure seemed like Double Dutch to me, which only added to my sense of confusion. Even after our pre-trial ordeal we still believed we were doing the right thing. The intimidation episode only reinforced my belief that Cooke would stop at nothing to win his freedom and that I had to fight him to the end.

The first day I had to take the witness stand was beyond awful. I had to face my abuser across the courtroom. He sat there impassive and emotionless throughout. The State Prosecutor asked me questions and I answered as best and as truthfully as I could. Sitting there opposite Cooke was just soul-destroying. Just being in the same room as him made my skin crawl. I have no doubt he secretly relished making each and every one of his victims relive their horrifying experiences in front of him. He compounded our suffering by making us publicly reveal the deepest torments of our lives. I felt utter contempt and disgust for him as he sat staring at me while I revealed to the judge and jury the things he had put me through as a little girl.

The memory of his voice would gnaw away at me after I'd left the courtroom. He had a soft voice, all whiney and whimpering, as if butter wouldn't melt in his mouth. He might have been an old man by this stage, but he was still a twisted, dirty pervert with an insatiable desire to destroy young lives. Being this close to him again heaped further torment on all the witnesses.

Cooke was very well versed in the law and used delaying tactics wherever possible. I felt so insignificant in that courtroom, so small and helpless, like someone standing looking at a huge tsunami just waiting for it to hit, not knowing when the impact would finally come and if I was going to survive. Mammy and Daddy came to the trial, and as grateful as I was for their support, in some ways their presence made it more painful for me. This was the first time they heard the full extent of what Cooke did to me in his house all those years ago. I had never been able to tell them all the details myself and it was truly horrendous for them to hear of it in a courtroom full of people. On one occasion, Mammy had to be carried from the courtroom when she heard the evidence about Cooke performing oral sex on me. She was so distraught at what she was hearing that it was awful for me to witness. All I wanted to do was go and comfort her. I was afraid to look my father in the eye, too, because I didn't want to see his hurt, anger and frustration.

I was the first to go into the witness box and I felt shame and embarrassment. My cheeks flushed with humiliation and I was scared that the jury might question why I hadn't ever told my parents the details of the abuse. It was very simple – I had always tried to spare them the hurt that I had been through. I had never divulged about the oral sex before because no one had ever asked me before. It hadn't even come into the equation until I had to go to the police and make a statement. But now I couldn't hide the awful realities of what happened and had to face a room full of strangers, my family and, worst still, Cooke, with the truth.

I also felt really stupid throughout the trial because I had to keep asking the Gardaí questions about court procedure. I felt inferior to everyone else in the courtroom, with a terrible fear of the unknown. But nothing could have prepared me for the cross-examination I underwent at the hands of Cooke's barrister Blaise O'Carroll. I fully understand that in a democratic and just society everyone should be entitled to a defence if they are accused of a crime. I also support the barristers who must defend an accused man or woman until they are found guilty. But I found the treatment I received from Cooke's counsel difficult to deal with and was totally shocked by some of his questions and the methods used to cross-examine me.

I would have loved the opportunity to present the jury with a photograph of myself at the age of seven and eight – the age when Cooke started to abuse me. It would have been a poignant reminder to the jury and everyone in the courtroom that the crimes for which he was on trial had not been committed against the adult standing before them.

They'd happened when I was a little girl, just like any child or grandchild of theirs.

I would try and answer questions without looking at anyone except the judge, but all the time I was aware that Mammy and Daddy were hearing these awful things. I could feel their pain, but there was one particular question that really staggered me. I was asked if I ever saw any wet substance in my underwear. I nearly passed out when I heard that.

On another occasion, the defence team handed out a diagram representing the layout of Cooke's house. The judge interrupted and said he had not been given one. I turned to him and said he could have mine because I didn't need it. I remembered exactly the way the house was. The defence team then started asking questions about the house. They wanted me to tell them its overall square footage and that of particular rooms. The whole situation was utterly ridiculous. I was in my mid-thirties at the time and didn't even know the square footage of my own home, so I was hardly going to know the square footage of a house seen when I was just seven years old. I felt that a lot of questions were posed purely to confuse or trip me up and felt afraid to answer them freely, which in turn made it seem as if I was being evasive. You see all these programmes on the television, courtroom dramas, which make everything there seem so glamorous and exciting. The real thing is nothing like that at all.

When my cross-examination was over, I was filled with relief and said a prayer of thanks to God that it was over. I hoped I would never have to experience anything like it again. Little did I know then what lay ahead of me.

I continued to go to court every day even though my evidence was over. I wanted to see the whole trial and to support the three remaining witnesses who still had to take the stand and give their evidence. When I sat and listened to their stories, they almost broke my heart. I would look at Eamonn Cooke and all that went through my head was, *You bastard.* He would see me watching him and would just stare back across the room without a flicker of emotion. He showed nothing on the surface, he kept his voice quiet and controlled, but I knew him well enough to realise that he was filled with rage inside.

The trial itself only lasted fifteen days but the delays and the pre-trial meant it was spread over about six weeks. I stayed in a Dublin hotel throughout that time. It was terribly lonely. Every night I would go back to my room and collapse into bed, emotionally shattered. I wanted to get to sleep as quickly as possible so the next day would come around quicker and take me one step closer to this whole ordeal being over.

One day back in court the prosecutors came up to me and said Cooke's defence wanted me back on the stand. I nearly collapsed with the shock. I just didn't think I could face it again and was terrified by the prospect. Luckily for me, the judge ruled that the defence team had had ample opportunity to question me previously and refused to let them put me back up there. I wanted to throw my arms around that judge and kiss him.

By far the worst part of the whole experience for me came almost at the end of the trial. Both sides were summing up the case before the judge and the jury. When it was Cooke's turn, Blaise O'Carroll took to his feet and in the middle of his speech announced that his client regarded me as 'evil'. He said that Cooke maintained I had made the whole thing up and got my friends to back me up. I just couldn't believe what I was hearing. My whole stomach churned and I felt bile rise into my throat. I had to run from the room, my stomach heaving in my distress. This was the trial of Eamonn Cooke, the most evil person I had ever met, and instead of him *I* was being called evil and a liar. It was such a low blow.

I have since spoken with defence barristers who have explained to me that in many cases they are assigned to represent Legal Aid cases and do not choose their defendants. I have also learned that they have to represent their clients to the best of their ability and must follow their clients' instructions so that should their client be convicted they can't be regarded as having been unfairly or poorly represented. This helped me enormously later in coming to terms with the tough line of questioning I'd faced in court, but it didn't make it any easier at the time.

The day we spent waiting to hear the jury's result was purgatory for us because we really had no idea how the verdict would fall. In a trial, you know you have told the truth but you don't know if the jurors have believed you. Our case seemed persuasive because two of the women involved had never met me or the other witness before the trial began. Such strong independent testimony surely had to be convincing. Cooke's *modus operandi*, however, had remained almost identical even though the offences had taken place a decade apart and in totally different areas. He had abused two of the victims in the 80s, myself and the fourth victim during the 70s. How could we possibly have made it up, which was what Cooke was trying to maintain we had done?

Nonetheless, we were sweating the whole time the jury was out because so much was at stake and we had already been through so much. My heart felt like it was beating out of my chest and I paced around the court building, not really knowing what to do with myself.

When the verdict came through and we heard that the jury had found Cooke guilty, we were just ecstatic. It had taken them just three hours to make their minds up. All six of us were sitting together when we heard the news and it was an amazing moment. We all cried and held one another, and our relief was beyond describing. At one stage during the proceedings, Cooke had tried to bar from the courtroom the two women whose cases had been shelved but he'd failed in his request and they were allowed to stay and hear the proceedings. Thank goodness they were there for the verdict, too.

In a very moving moment as I left the courtroom, a member of the jury came up and hugged me. The woman squeezed me hard and said, 'I believed you from the moment you took the stand.' I burst into tears and wept in her arms because it meant so much to me to be believed. Her words will never, ever leave me. They were so important for me, and remain so. But while our victory was brilliant for me, it was tainted for the two women whose cases were never heard. Even though they were genuinely delighted that Cooke had been convicted on the charges against us, there was still a sense of personal loss for them.

One of them cried when she said, 'That bastard will never serve a single day's time for the crimes he committed against me.' It tore me up to witness their grief.

Other members of the jury also came up to us, saying we had been very brave and now we should try and get on with our lives. They all said what a bastard Eamonn Cooke was and sympathised with us all for what we had been through. When we left the court, we went out with the police team to celebrate our victory – and most of the jury came with us! It was quite unusual but we were delighted to have them along. It was a long night and we were in no hurry to finish celebrating.

The trial finished in December 2002 and Cooke was sent to jail as a convicted paedophile. But it was not until March 2003 that he was due to be sentenced. When I returned to the courtroom that day it was packed to the rafters. This had been an extremely high-profile case since the defendant had been very well known in Ireland for decades. It had also caused shockwaves in the same way that the revelations of the child abuse rife within the Catholic Church had done.

I sat down before sentencing began and, to my horror, saw Cooke coming towards me. He had not been restrained in the dock but been allowed to roam the courtroom even though he had been remanded in custody since his conviction. Now he had the gall to come and sit right beside me. He wasn't even flanked by prison officers, and all of a sudden was sitting arm to arm with me. I froze in panic, unable to breathe, unable even to squeak out a call for help. People noticed but just seemed to wait and see if he would be moved, but none of the court officials realised what was going on because the room was so busy.

I felt the contents of my stomach rise up at the stench of him. He was so close I could hear him draw breath. I didn't know what to do but fortunately at that moment my husband walked in and instantly saw what Cooke had done. Derek strode over and placed himself between us. The man I loved most in the world sat alongside the man I most hated. It was a bizarre and disturbing situation and I complained about it afterwards. It should never have been allowed to occur.

Before sentence was passed, the court heard my own victim impact statement and the victim impact report prepared by my clinical psychologist, Michael Dempsey. His report read as follows:

At your request I interviewed Ms Kennedy-McGuinness on 5 February 2003 for the purpose of preparing this report. I had previously prepared a report dated 17 November 2002 in relation to her delay in reporting to the Gardaí the sexual abuse by Mr Cooke on her. Assessment in November 2002 indicated that she was suffering from symptoms of Post Traumatic Stress Disorder to a severe degree as a consequence of the sexual abuse. Ms Kennedy-McGuinness reported that following her interview with me in November, flashbacks to the abuse and nightmares became more frequent. This was to be expected as discussing the details of the abuse and its consequences frequently retraumatises victims. She reported that she was traumatised further by the trial and especially having to give evidence over two days at the trial. She reported that she had had to give evidence on a previous occasion in relation to Mr Cooke intimidating her and she had found these occasions distressing.

On interview, she was experiencing a diffuse sense of anger over the abuse and aspects of the trial. She reported that at one stage during the trial she had vomited as she felt her character was being attacked. She reported that she finds it difficult to switch off from thinking about the abuse since the ending of the trial. She continues to experience the symptoms of intrusion and avoidance that characterise PTSD. She reported that she had woken up recently and felt Mr Cooke was in the bedroom. She is now getting visions of him in the dark and she is distressed by these events. She wakes up sweating and has nightmares about his abuse. Here Ms Kennedy-McGuinness is describing symptoms of intrusion that are central to Post Traumatic Stress Disorder. She tries to avoid thinking about the abuse. She reported that following the trial she isolated herself and hid in her house for some weeks. Her business has suffered as a result and she reported that she lost interest in her business. Her relationship with her husband continues to suffer as a result of the abuse . . . [S]he is reporting a severe degree of depression.

She reported that she will feel safer if Mr Cooke goes to prison.

In conclusion, Ms Kennedy-McGuinness is currently suffering from Post Traumatic Stress Disorder and severe depression as a consequence of the sexual abuse. Having to attend professionals such as myself, make statements to the Gardaí and give evidence in court has served to exacerbate her symptoms. In my opinion, the prognosis for recovery is guarded and will depend on a number of factors. The sentence imposed is one factor. Additionally, she would benefit from psychological treatment for her symptoms – however, as avoidance is a core facet of PTSD, she may avoid treatment for her symptoms. In any event, I would anticipate she would require psychological treatment over an extended period of time.

It was a fair assessment of my health and it helped me to acknowledge the severity of the damage Cooke had inflicted on me. My own impact assessment read far more simply:

The first thing I would like to say is that I can never fully explain to people in words the impact of the damage I have suffered over the years in relation to the sexual abuse by Eamonn Cooke and more recently the court case. At times, the effect of the abuse has been horrendous. I never fully realised what he did to me until I got older. I got on with my life the best I could, firstly with the help of my family, who always made me feel loved and secure as a person. For a long while I thought I had done something wrong, but my parents reassured me that it was never my fault. Secondly, my husband restored my confidence in myself as a woman. I had never felt this way as a teenager when I began to realise what Cooke had done to me. There have been many times I felt I could not cope and these are the people who have helped me keep my life together.

There was one particular time when I read an article in a newspaper, quoting Cooke about child abuse and he was saying how terrible it was to take a child's innocence away. He had taken mine away. When I saw that article I knew he had no remorse for that, nor will he ever. If he felt any shame or compassion, he would not have put his victims through the six weeks of hell we have endured throughout this trial. At one stage, it felt like I was the person on trial and I was turned inside out by Cooke's legal team. It is an experience I never want to go through again. I had to listen to his terrible lies and accusations against me and I felt my character was being assassinated. I felt it was stooping a bit low to call me evil. Cooke will never do the time in prison that I have suffered in my life. He took a part of me away that I can never restore. I will never know the person I might have become if Cooke hadn't abused me. His sentencing means a lot to me in many ways and as far as I am concerned, the longer the better. I will feel a lot safer knowing he is behind bars unable to do to any other children what he did to me and others.

Eventually, Cooke's sick past caught up with him and I passionately believe we are just the tip of the iceberg as far as the number of his victims is concerned. I hope to sleep much better knowing that the 'Cookie Monster' is no more.

Cooke was sentenced to a total of ten years for a long list of crimes against his four victims. He was sixty-six years old when he was sentenced on thirty-three separate charges of child sex abuse. Mr Justice John Quirke said Cooke had showed no remorse for the damage inflicted on his victims, and that he himself had no doubt the correct verdict had been delivered. He added that he could find no mitigating circumstances in any of the convictions.

The judge had been brilliant and we were all over the moon with his ruling. There was one comment someone made to me that I will never forget. The person was American and, after the sentencing, they turned to me and said, 'Honey, if he was at home, he would be fried.' We could only live in hope, I mused. But, given our legal system, I genuinely felt that justice, at long last, had been served. Cooke was proven to be the pervert we had always known him to be and we were vindicated in our fight for justice. It had taken three years and now I felt the time had come for me to move on with my life. I had no idea that for me it was far from over.

16

After the trial I resumed my former life but didn't feel the overpowering sense of elation and liberation I had imagined I would experience once Cooke was jailed. I was still struggling with the injustice done to the two victims whose cases had been ruled out of the trial. That had landed him one very undeserved victory. While we had been lucky to get justice in the end, we had all been through a hard time during the trial and I suppose there was an inevitable sense of deflation and exhaustion afterwards. I was trying to get my life back to normal, but how could I do that with no sense of direction or support? It had been acknowledged in court that I was suffering from Post Traumatic Stress Disorder, and yet no safety net had been provided for me or any of the others during or after the trial. While I was doing my best to pick up the pieces, I knew I didn't feel right. Where are you supposed to put all those tumultuous feelings you have experienced in court when you leave the courtroom and return to your family?

I began to spiral back into depression again. I found it difficult to talk to anyone about it, but I started panicking that Cooke was going to come after me once he was released from prison. The nightmares took hold of me once more and I was wracked with guilt for not feeling more euphoric at Cooke's ten-year conviction.

I realised I was angry because there was no one there to help me after the trial, when I felt I needed it the most. Cooke, on the other hand, was offered all the help available in prison, including a rehabilitation programme, even though he refused it because he continued to maintain he was an innocent man – a calculated decision on his part because to accept help would have been a public admission of his guilt. There was no question that he was an extra-ordinarily astute, smart and manipulative deviant, who had for far too long managed to evade the law.

The six women who'd experienced that trial had grown very close while it lasted, but when it was over even we found it difficult to talk to each other – it was almost as if we were all trying to bury the memories once again, shove them safely back in their boxes.

I remember going to my doctor's one day with a bad chest infection and telling her I felt unwell. She knew nothing of what I had been through but must have sensed that all was not well because as I was walking out the door, she called after me, 'Is everything okay with you, Siobhan?'

'Well, actually, it's not,' I replied.

She asked what was wrong and I said that I felt utterly exhausted. I told her about the trial then and about my worries that I didn't think I was handling it too well. I wasn't in as extreme a frame of mind as I had been in past years, but I knew I was heading back in that direction. I talked to her about my feelings and told her about the victim impact report that had been prepared on me.

'Siobhan, I think you are close to a breakdown and complete mental exhaustion. I really think you need to see a professional about this,' she told me.

She was shocked that I had never been offered any help before and recommended that I went to see someone at Newcastle Hospital, a psychiatric centre that she thought would be able to help me. I agreed to go. The doctors there were great. I didn't realise how low I was until I got there and they told me I was suffering from exhaustion and depression and was heading for a breakdown. They advised that I should go into hospital for rest and treatment. Initially, I resisted this because I was worried about leaving my family again so soon after the trial, but eventually I knew it was something I had to do.

I spent two weeks in Newcastle Hospital where I was finally cared for and treated properly. For the first time I began to feel different, as if I had a real purpose in life. I had lots of one-to-one counselling, but couldn't help but feel a bit of a fraud while I was there because I met a lot of people with severe mental health problems, like schizophrenia and manic depression. I could still put on a smile before the rest of the world even though I had been diagnosed with depression.

Perhaps old habits die hard, but I took the treatment seriously and tried to make the most of the help that was being offered to me. I loved being able just to have the time to look after myself, and slept properly while I was there, for the first time in many years. I was put on a course of medication to help me and eventually left Newcastle in

August 2003. To this day I am still an outpatient there, the doctors making sure that I stay well and look after myself.

When I returned home, I could feel myself getting stronger every day until one day I had a phone call from one of the other witnesses in the trial. She told me she had read an article in the newspaper about Cooke. He had been granted leave to appeal his conviction.

I was stunned by the news and phoned the Garda who confirmed the forthcoming appeal. I was dismayed that I had only learned about it through hearsay and a newspaper article, after everything we had done to put him away. My freedom from the nightmare of Eamonn Cooke had not lasted long.

Over the next couple of years there were numerous bids by him to overrule his conviction, but each appeal was turned down on legal grounds. I had to attend numerous High Court hearings while Cooke pursued his bids for freedom. He also continued using intimidating behaviour.

I attended one hearing at the High Court with another victim, a representative from One In Four called Deirdre Fitzpatrick, and Mammy. What happened on this occasion was as shocking as the day he'd sat next to me at his sentencing.

Cooke was still in custody and when he first arrived in court was taken to the dock. He looked as disgusting as ever, though none of us passed comment on this aloud. We said it all with our eyes and our skin crawled with revulsion. It was a lengthy procedure and at certain times we'd sit outside the courtroom in a little annexe. It was a confined space that would seat no more than about five people. We were huddled there for a short break from the proceedings when all of a sudden Cooke walked out of the court and sat down right in the middle of us all. At first none of us said anything, too shocked by his audacity. His other victim got up and walked off first, then Mammy stormed off. Deirdre and I sat on defiantly for a few moments before we also got up and walked away. What was most shocking of all to us was that he was supposed to be in custody and yet he was free to come and deliberately sit among his victims. He was supposed to be handcuffed and supervised at all times and yet he was walking around the court building like a free man.

We were so disgusted that we complained and were advised to write to the Governor of the prison where he was being held. We did so and received a reply saying that he was satisfied that Cooke had been supervised at all times, which was certainly not the case. It was shoddy behaviour on the part of the court and the prison service. Cooke not only tried to frighten and unnerve us once again, he could have tried to harm us. We could, furthermore, have harmed him if we had been that way inclined. It was another example of Cooke trying to intimidate his victims in the very place where they were seeking redress against him. One in Four was so dismayed and alarmed by what had happened that they filed a complaint and a full report on the incident.

Cooke lost his appeal that day and was taken back to prison where he continued to plot and scheme. He was determined not to give up, though, and in May 2006 finally succeeded. He walked free from jail on what emerged as a legal technicality. An appeal judge said it was no fault of the victims or the police that Cooke had been released from prison. The appeal court's judgement ruled that Cooke's conviction was unsafe because neither the defence, the prosecution nor the judge had issued a warning to the jury about the difficulties that can arise in cases where there is a long period of time between the alleged offences taking place and the subsequent court hearing. A precedent had been set at an earlier unrelated trial in Ireland that stated the court had a duty to warn juries in such cases of difficulties arising from factors such as memory loss or the ability to recall defence witnesses. It was a procedural error that Cooke used to his advantage. He managed to exploit the system and win his freedom because the State had no choice but to adhere to the very letter of its own law.

I was completely devastated to see him walk free after everything we had endured. The only way forward from here was if the DPP decided they would go for a retrial, but there were mixed opinions as to whether this was going to happen. I was also terrified that now Cooke was free I would personally suffer the repercussions, and I felt completely unprotected.

Before the end of his appeal hearing and subsequent release, Gerry Kelly had approached the prosecutors to ask if they could request that Cooke be held in custody until a decision had been made by the State about conducting a retrial. Unfortunately, this request was not put before the judge and Cooke was a free man once again, able to live at large in the middle of an innocent community in Dublin, within easy reach of more unsuspecting children and their families.

At the end of the appeal, as Cooke walked from the

courtroom, I went up to Pat McCarthy and Isobel Kennedy who were acting for the prosecution and I told them that I truly believed they had done everything in their power to keep this man locked up. I thanked them for all the work they had done. There was general belief in his guilt, but we also knew the DPP might be reluctant to go for a retrial because two of the women who had been witnesses with me in the first trial had already indicated they could not face going through another one. That potentially left just two of us to go back up against Cooke.

I knew that it was hugely expensive to mount a criminal trial, but to my mind no amount of money could equate to the price of a child's safety. I passionately believed that everything possible should be done to get this man back in jail where he belonged. I suspected, too, that the Irish people would wish no expense to be spared to ensure that Cooke was never again allowed to exercise his deviant nature against young children.

Those of us who had had the misfortune to come into contact with him knew without doubt that he would never change. As a predatory sexual offender, his desire for children would not diminish, no matter how much time he spent in prison. I made my position very clear before I left court that day. I was prepared to face a retrial and give evidence against Eamonn Cooke for a second time. Pat and Isobel, who had performed brilliantly at the first trial, were crestfallen and said how sorry they were about the outcome, but I stressed again that I hoped the DPP would go forward with a retrial. I was not prepared to let it go, I told them. I think it was with that last declaration that I found something inside of me, some source of strength, that would guide me through. I felt certain this was not an end to it.

Just a few paragraphs in the newspaper marked Cooke's release back into society. The report did not name him or carry a photograph. The headline ran: '*Legal Blunder Forces Child Sex Retrial*'. The report continued:

> A sixty-nine-year-old man who was serving a ten-year jail term for a string of child sex crimes will face a retrial after his convictions were quashed yesterday. The pensioner was sentenced in March 2003 after being found guilty of thirty-three offences — including attempted rape, and indecent assault — on four girls under the age of fifteen. Yesterday the Court of Criminal Appeal heard that the man's legal team was challenging the convictions because the original judge had failed to warn the jury about the 'dangers inherent in a trial which takes place many years after the offences alleged and the difficulties which such a trial creates for the defence'. Judge Nicholas Kearns said: 'Lawyers on both sides of the case had omitted to warn the jury about difficulties about allegations dating back many years.' He told the court: 'It was a most unfortunate omission by counsel, having regard to the impeccable handling of this case at all stages by the learned trial judge over a period of several weeks. However, without laying down in any detail the nature or extent of the warning which should

have been given in this case, this court is satisfied that some sort of warning was essential and that, without such warning, the conviction herein cannot be regarded as safe.'

In fact, a decision had not yet been declared by the DPP as to whether Cooke would definitely face a retrial, even though it remained a possibility. A few weeks went by and my sleep pattern was all over the place but I didn't allow myself to slip back into the deep depression that had overcome me many times before. I recalled the words of the woman juror in the first trial, about how she had believed me from the moment I gave evidence, and that gave me a slither of hope to hang on to. Soon after, I was asked if there was any way I could put into writing what I had said to Pat and Isobel on the day Cooke walked free. On 8 June 2006, this is what I wrote to the DPP:

The decision of the court to free Eamonn Cooke in May has left me devastated. This man has perpetrated gross sexual acts of indecency on myself, and others, over a long period of time, and has shown no remorse. It is sickening to think that he uses our judicial system to manipulate himself back into society. I went to hell and back to help the State secure a conviction against this animal and I am willing to go through a retrial to help myself, his other victims and potential victims, as I believe his depravity knows no bounds. The DPP now have a choice to fight and keep this evil man away from society, but most importantly, a chance to keep him as a convicted paedophile and on the Sex Offenders' Register where he belongs. Six of his victims went forward on a pre-trial and two cases were shelved, not because he was not guilty, but because he found legal technicalities to prevent these charges from going forward to trial. At the trial four victims gave evidence. The criminal case lasted for six weeks and we were cross-examined at great length. At one stage I felt that I was on trial and had to remind myself countless times that I was the injured party. When Mr Blaise O'Carroll was summing up the defendant's case, he made reference to me as being 'evil'. I had committed no crime but was made to feel that I was the criminal for speaking out and seeking justice against this monster. During the trial, I was not allowed any legal representation to speak for me, as the prosecution barrister is only there to represent the State. I feel that the 'system' is weighed heavily in favour of the accused and this is a major reason why other victims are afraid to come forward. I feel that a retrial is necessary to prevent this habitual sexual predator from claiming more victims. I feel the depravity of this man knows no bounds and I believe the DPP must fight to keep this evil man away from society and on the Sex Offenders' Register where he belongs.

I hope after reading this letter you will understand why I feel it is so important that this man should not be allowed to walk free, without a conviction, for the heinous crimes he has perpetrated on so many young and innocent children, as I was when he abused me. I am willing to face the stress and trauma of a retrial to prevent Cooke from using legal loopholes to worm his way out of his conviction, leaving him free to stalk and abuse more victims.

Yours honestly,

Mrs Siobhan Kennedy-McGuinness

It took me a long time to write my letter because I didn't know how to put my feelings down on to paper, so I just tried to speak from the heart, even though I know it wasn't couched in highbrow legal terms. Many people feared the DPP would not proceed with a further trial, but until we heard their decision, I had to keep hoping.

Late in the summer of 2006, I got a phone call from Gerry Kelly, telling me that the DPP had decided to go for a retrial. I was gob-smacked. On the one hand I was absolutely delighted because I was being given a chance to try and keep this pervert behind bars. On the other, I just looked to the heavens and muttered, *Oh my God, here we go again.* I knew this was going to be yet another huge upheaval for my family, albeit one worth suffering. All the victims who were eligible to give evidence were asked if they were prepared to go through another trial. At one stage it looked pretty grim, as I was the only one prepared to do battle with Cooke again. Even though it would be extremely hard without the others, though, I was prepared to fight on alone because I knew I had the truth on my side. I completely understood why the other women had decided not to come forward again as witnesses. It was an entirely personal decision for each one of us, and for some it was all just too much. Emotionally they had thrown in the towel because they didn't feel capable of facing the ordeal again, and who could blame them for that? I still had the strength to continue. I don't know where that strength came from but I had started something, and I wanted to see it through to the very end.

Eventually, a second woman decided she too would go forward again and I was delighted with her decision. It meant I would not have to fight Cooke alone and was news I had been longing to hear.

One Sunday, I was working in my shop unit at the market as usual when who should turn up again but Cooke? In a way, I had been half expecting him to pull a stunt like this, but I still got a jolt when I saw him standing there in front of me. I was at my little music shop and he was standing just a few yards away. He didn't have any children with him this time. Instead, he had his mobile phone and started to video me with it. He held the phone up and recorded my every move. It took me back to the days when I was just a tiny girl being filmed by him as I danced in his garden. It sent a shiver down my spine but although I was very scared, I knew I had to attract attention to him.

He was free on bail awaiting his second trial, but I had had his bail revoked once before and was prepared to try and do so again. I shouted to a security guard.

'Excuse me,' I hollered as loud as I could manage. 'Excuse me . . . this man here is a paedophile. He hurts children and he shouldn't be here. Can you please have him removed?' I shouted it as loud as I could, but my voice was hoarse with fear. I could feel the colour rising up my face and neck. Why had no one come running to my assistance? Didn't they know what this man was capable of?

Cooke stood there as if he hadn't a bother in the world. The security guard eventually went up to him and told him he would have to leave. Cooke kept saying that he didn't know what I was talking about. That he hadn't known I even worked in the market. That was absolute nonsense and we both knew it. He eventually left and I asked the security guard if he would back me up when I reported what had happened. He said he would.

I phoned Gerry Kelly but didn't manage to get hold of him immediately. Eventually we spoke, and I stumbled and stuttered over my words as I tried to explain what had happened.

From that day on until the trial started, I was ultra-careful about my personal security, even down to checking under my car for devices before I left home in the morning. It sounds ridiculous but I never underestimated Cooke. If I was driving, I would even go round roundabouts several times to make sure I was not being followed and constantly checked my rear-view and wing mirrors. I was always very nervous when I went to work in case he tried anything there again. I was even suspicious of some of my customers, especially if I didn't recognise them. I would wonder if Cooke had sent them in to spy on me or unnerve me in some way. Those who knew what he was capable of didn't think I was being paranoid.

Gerry called again in December 2006 and told me he had

some good news. In fact, he said it was better than that. He said he had an early Christmas present for me because Pat and Isobel had been granted the case for the State again. The other witness and I were over the moon at this. These two knew Cooke so well by now that it gave them the edge over any other prosecutors who might have been assigned. They were undoubtedly the best pair for the job, whereas if we had been given new prosecutors, we would have had to start from scratch. Pat and Isobel already knew all the defendant's devious ways and it put them ahead of the game before we'd even started.

Cooke's second trial was due to start at the Central Criminal Court in Dublin on 29 January 2007. Inevitably, there were delays. In this instance, there was no trial judge immediately available on that date. In early-February, the retrial finally got underway before a female judge, Ms Justice Maureen Clark. Cooke was charged with forty-two counts of indecent assault for various sexual crimes committed against two children during the 1970s.

I felt much stronger than when I had given evidence at the first trial. I had changed as a person, besides learning a lot more about the law and how the legal system worked. I can't say I wasn't scared, because I was, but I didn't have that fear of the unknown that had dogged me during the first case. I was also a lot calmer and less angry. The psychiatric treatment I had been receiving had made a huge impact on my life, for the better. In addition, I was getting help from two amazing voluntary organisations – the Rape Crisis Centre and One In Four. Breda Allen from the rape centre phoned me every single day throughout that trial, to offer moral and emotional support. Deirdre Fitzpatrick from One in Four was also there for me throughout everything, including giving advice on legal matters, so I was in a far better place than when I'd first faced Cooke in court.

As well as these people and my family supporting me, I also had Gerry and his team of detectives who consistently offered advice and support to both myself and the other woman giving evidence. I think they were surprised to see how much I had changed since the last trial, especially when I stood before the judge and jury to give evidence. Everyone knew Cooke was guilty but the police officers were nervous that this time there were only two witnesses against him. They hadn't banked on how strong, determined and convincing those two witnesses would be when they took the stand for the second time. Afterwards Gerry told me that all the police thought we witnesses had been amazing. In fact, throughout the whole trial, I didn't feel nearly as overwhelmed as I had previously. Raw experience had taught me a lot. This time I amazed myself.

During my evidence, I described how I'd taken an overdose after failing to get help to deal with the aftermath of the abuse. The jury were told that it had taken place after I'd read the newspaper article about Cooke campaigning against the Church on behalf of his wife who'd reported being sexually abused by a priest.

'I couldn't deal with him asking how someone could take a child's innocence when he had taken mine. Both a GP and a priest told me just to get on with my life. That was when I took the overdose,' I explained to another roomful of strangers.

Before long Cooke began his old tricks again and started to try and delay proceedings. The trial had been underway a few days when it broke for the weekend. The following Monday, Cooke hobbled into court on a pair of crutches. His defence barrister, Mr Niall Durnin (Senior Counsel), addressed the judge and told her that his client had suffered a fall over the weekend. As a result of injuries to his pelvis, Cooke had been placed on morphine for pain relief and was therefore worried he was not fit to continue with the trial. He argued he would not be able to follow the proceedings properly because of the strong medication he was taking. To me, it just seemed like another ploy by Cooke to delay the trial as well as a bid to play the sympathy card before the jury. He was doing a good job of acting the frail old man but it cut no ice with those of us who knew his game plan. There had been several recent trials where leniency had been shown to offenders because they were old. They weren't linked to Cooke's case or necessarily paedophiles, just defendants who had come before the court in old age. In one instance a man in his seventies was given a suspended sentence because of his age, but this outraged me because paedophiles don't care what age their victims are when they are abusing them, so why should our courts show leniency when justice eventually catches up with them?

The judge, however, treated Cooke's concerns seriously and delayed the trial so that he could be seen by a doctor in Dublin to assess whether he was fit to continue. The outcome was that, on the doctor's advice, the judge directed he was well enough to continue; she had given him the benefit of the doubt to ensure he received fair treatment, but none of us believed it had been anything more than a disruptive delaying tactic.

When the trial re-started, Cooke complained that his injuries made it uncomfortable for him to sit all day on the seat in the dock and so the judge decided to ask court officials to provide a special padded chair for him to use. I remember Mammy asking the guard at the time if it was possible to get him an electric one. It was typical of her black humour, but it made us giggle all the same.

Cooke was provided with a special orthopaedic chair, which was placed outside the dock at the end of the public bench where we would sit to hear the proceedings. This meant that every time he came into the courtroom, he had to hobble past us as we sat on the bench. It was probably a very juvenile thing to do, but one day the other witness and I deliberately stretched out our legs on the floor in front of us so that he would have to struggle over them on his crutches. I didn't feel any pity, despite his trying to portray himself as an injured old man. When the judge referred to Cooke's pubic bone injury, I said it couldn't have happened to a better *buachaill* (pronounced 'bookel' – an Irish term for a lad). It was just a shame it hadn't happened thirty years earlier.

At times the trial lurched into the realms of farce, like the occasion when Cooke was questioned about his personal hygiene and whether or not he wore underwear. He had never worn underwear under his trousers when he'd abused us, and we testified to this in court. We also described how dirty he was and that he smelled of BO because he didn't wash. When he was asked in court about his cleanliness, his face was deadpan.

'Now how would I find the time to have a bath?' he replied. The expressions on the jurors' faces were a picture. I am not sure they could quite believe what they'd heard. Cooke also admitted that he rarely wore underwear, but said sometimes he wore boxer shorts in the winter if it was cold. To my recollection, boxer shorts were not even around in the 1970s. Had the circumstances not been so serious and sinister this whole line of questioning would have seemed hilarious.

What really hit me during the retrial was just how little I'd been when these crimes were committed against me. One of the most distressing aspects about facing him in the second trial was something very close to home. My daughter was now seven years old, the very age I was when Cooke first abused me. She had only just been born when I'd started my journey towards justice. Seven years on Cooke still dominated my life. It broke my heart to look at her innocent face, the spitting image of mine at that age. I couldn't stop crying when I looked at how small and vulnerable she was and realised I had been like that once – and Cooke had taken full advantage of it. I wondered then how Mammy had ever coped with what Cooke had done to me.

The trial still wasn't easy, even though I felt stronger and was more familiar with the workings of the law. I tried to hold on to the fact that all twelve of the jury had found him guilty the first time around, and although we were down to only two witnesses this time, we still had a good chance of reconvicting him. But in my heart I struggled to believe that Cooke would go back to prison, if found guilty for a second time. As he had already served almost four years for the first trial and there were only two of us testifying against him this time, he could end up walking out a free man.

Finally, in March 2007, a jury reconvicted Cooke who was found guilty of all forty-two charges of sexual assault made against him. This time it took them just two hours to return their verdict on the majority of the charges against the accused. It was yet another monumental milestone for justice. For the second time, the man who tried so hard to ruin our lives had been found guilty. For the second time, I thought the judge had done brilliantly and shown fairness to everyone. She also went to great lengths to sum up with crystal clarity for the jury, clearly not wishing to leave any grounds for another appeal. It was an extremely draining process but if I had to do it again I would. The judge remarked in particular on my evidence when I described how, as a child, I was scared my gran could see me from heaven in Cooke's bed. She was also struck by the horrendous imagery of him picking up two naked little girls, one under each arm, and taking them into his bed. It meant a lot to me to know I had been able to express my case with such an impact and that she recognised how difficult the whole experience had been.

There were a lot of women in court that day – not just the two who had secured his conviction for a second time. There were a lot of family members, as well as other victims of Cooke's who had not been able to give evidence against him. When he was taken back into custody there was a huge collective sigh of relief that he was off the streets again.

When he was gone, I went and thanked every single one of the jurors for their belief in us and we chatted for a while. I had a strong sense of *déjà vu* because, just like in the first trial, they all said they'd believed us from the outset, which filled me with a great sense of relief.

When we walked out of the courtroom about nine women just hugged and held each other and cried. All victims of Cooke, we had finally found some assuagement after our long and exhausting quest for justice. You could feel the emotion coming off everyone, and when we linked with one another in solidarity it was as if an electric charge ran through us and united us inextricably for a few seconds. We will probably never share that same sense of unity again but we will always remember it. Several minutes later, the judge walked from the courtroom and caught sight of the women still holding on to each other. As I looked up I glimpsed her smiling at us, sharing with us for the briefest of moments a sense that this was a victory for real justice and not just the courtroom kind.

I think everyone in court that day shared an unspoken sense of joy that Cooke had been sent back to jail, from the court usher to the prison guards. Gerry Kelly and his police team were truly thrilled. When I thought back to the first time I'd walked into that police station to give my statement, I was truly staggered by the distance I had come. It was a traumatic journey at times, and definitely not made any easier by the difficult legal system, but the one thing I have come away with is the highest regard for the police team who accompanied me. They were at all times dedicated and professional, and I can never thank them enough for their commitment.

I don't blame the police for the system they have to work

within but politicians need to make changes to help ease the judicial process for victims of abuse. They need to provide more money to improve facilities for all witnesses who come forward.

I also took away with me the highest regard for the prosecution team, as I did for Mr Niall Durnin. As Cooke's second defence barrister, he had a hard task to carry out but performed his role with great professionalism at all times.

As for Cooke, nothing surprised me anymore about him and the lengths he would go to, including the description he gave to the judge and jury about how he had built an underground bunker in which to store his belongings. He said it was where he had stored the tape recording of me made when I was still a child. He outlined how he would slide down a manmade chute to access the bunker. I have no idea what the jury must have made of this revelation. Here was a seventy-year-old man volunteering information to the court that he had created secret storage bunkers under the ground. It seemed an outlandish claim, but knowing Cooke it didn't shock me. Gardaí confirmed the existence of his bunker when they revealed they had uncovered and searched it during their investigation of him but the tape recording of me was never found. Cooke never denied the existence of the tape. He had no reason to because his claim was that I was lying during the interview all those years ago, even though two independent juries would eventually establish that it was Cooke who was the liar.

Cooke is a clever man but some of his evidence must have sounded ludicrous to the jury. One of the witnesses gave evidence to say that she believed Cooke smoked Rothmans cigarettes. He went on to try and paint her as a liar because he said Rothmans was the only brand of cigarettes he would never smoke because he hated them. He was challenged by prosecution counsel and asked that if he ran out of cigarettes, would he refuse a Rothmans but accept any other brand of smoke. He said yes. It made him appear pedantic and petty in a bid to make his point about suggesting the witness was lying and I don't believe the jury bought it for a moment.

The more Cooke threw at us, the harder we fought back. The final vindication for me came on Friday 30 March 2007 when Ms Justice Maureen Clark sentenced a then seventy-year-old Cooke to ten years in jail. She told the court that she had wanted to send him to prison for one year for each of the forty-two sexual assaults, but her powers did not permit her to do so. Instead, she handed down the maximum jail term she was able to.

Everyone in that courtroom was profoundly surprised and overjoyed by the judge's decision. It was better than anything in our wildest dreams. All I had hoped for was to uphold the original conviction and keep him on the Sex Offenders' Register, but now he was back in jail with a substantial increase in his prison term given the years he had already served.

As his sentence was read out, the victim at the centre of Cooke's earlier firebomb attack shouted out, 'I hope you rot in hell.'

The judge addressed all the women at the back of the court when she said, 'It has been a long five or six years for all of you, and maybe a lifetime for some. I hope today gives you some sense of finality and that you never have to appear in court again.'

We were fortunate to have two wise judges conducting the trials who acted with the utmost professionalism at all times. They restored my faith in a justice system I had almost given up on.

Cooke's previous convictions were then read out in court. Gerry Kelly told Pat McCarthy that Cooke had eight previous convictions spanning fifty-one years, including shooting with intent, arson, malicious damage and contempt of court. He said Cooke had received a four-year suspended sentence for an arson attack on one of the complainants in the 2002 trial.

Cooke continued to deny all the charges on which he was convicted, claiming the allegations were made merely to blacken his name. His counsel Mr Durnin said that since Cooke was 'maintaining his position', he was unable to offer any mitigation apart from his client's personal circumstances. He asked Ms Justice Clark to take into consideration Cooke's age and the fact that he had been prevented access to his children since his arrest and that fact was 'weighing very heavily on him'.

17

After both of Cooke's trials, there was significant media interest in his convictions, on the television, radio, and in the national newspapers. It had been something of a shock to the public to discover that one of the best-known radio personalities in the country was guilty of such heinous crimes. But while the case was widely reported, the identities of all the women involved in the proceedings remained anonymous. The law states that victims of sex abuse cannot be identified unless they waive their right to anonymity.

One particular article was particularly poignant in its description of myself and the other witness as we gave our evidence during the second trial. Reporter Louise Hogan had witnessed us detailing the abuse we'd suffered to the jury and described in the *Irish Independent* how we had suffered a lifetime of torment after the paedophile's cruel attacks on us. I think her description really captured some of the emotion in that courtroom as we were forced to relive our abuse in front of Cooke. Her report read:

The victim's voice wavered as she described her

pain as 'simply a drop in the ocean' of torment caused to other children by the founder of the illegal Radio Dublin station. The voices of the two victims — one strong, the other trembling — rang out clear across the courtroom as they described how their lives were destroyed as children in the 1970s at the hands of Eamonn Cooke. Sitting across from the wizened old man who held his crutches tightly as he stared determinedly ahead, they warned that he was a sexual predator.

'He is motivated by sexual desire for children; that is what he is, that is what he has always been, and that is what he always will be,' one woman said. 'My pain is simply a drop in the ocean of the pain that man has created in people's lives.'

After the seventy year old was handed down a ten-year jail term, their faces filled with delight.

'I feel totally at peace at the moment. I didn't expect ten years. It has been a very, very long road,' one witness said.

Family members sitting close together at the back of the court shed silent tears, grasped tissues and closed their eyes as the horrific assaults were detailed. As innocent children they [the victims] had been groomed to accept his deviant sexual behaviour as normal. It was only much later that they were able to recognise they were the innocent victims of a paedophile's grooming, where secrecy and shame had become the norm, the judge said.

When I returned home to my family after the second trial it was a huge relief, but I remained unsettled for a while. All I wanted to do was curl up and go to sleep but I had my husband and children to look after. After another lengthy separation because of the trial, I took comfort from being back with them.

Derek and I spent a week cocooned at home with the children and it was bliss. For so many weeks, the Four Courts in Dublin and an anonymous hotel bedroom had been my home. Derek had done a superb job of keeping family life going as normal. While my family turned up at court to support me every day, his rallied round to help share the load of caring for our kids. I was adamant that I didn't want my children to miss one day of school because of Cooke. I might have been away, but I had fantastic support at home to make sure my family continued to function as normally as possible.

I now had to try to explain to my children why I had been away from them for so long. I didn't want to frighten them or tell them things they were too young to understand, but I knew I had to find a way of talking to them about what I had been through. It was easier with my older sons, Glenn and Cian, because they were mature enough to have a grasp of what had happened in my life. It was much tougher with the two youngest children.

It's hard enough being a mother at the best of times. Everyone who has been there knows that there are no rulebooks on how best to bring up kids. I first broached talking to them about things before the retrial. Derek and I were sitting in front of a big coal fire one night with them when I said, 'Listen, kids, there's something I need to talk to you about. I need to go away for a while to sort some business. I just want you to know that there are some bold people in the world who sometimes do bad things. We all have neighbours, and some neighbours are good and some neighbours are bad. When Mammy was a little girl, I lived beside a man who was not so good. He was bold and he hurt me.'

'How did he hurt you, Mammy, did he hit you?' Ryan replied.

'No, he didn't hit me but he did put his hands somewhere on my body where he shouldn't have.'

It was a very hard conversation to have without being too graphic. I had already tried to explain to all my kids about protecting themselves. One of my sons had begun what they called a 'Stay Safe' programme in school, which was designed to explain in gentle terms about keeping away from perverts. The mantra of the programme was: 'Never let a touch be a secret.' I thought this was brilliant and a long way from anything I had ever learned in school. I used it as a basis on which to build my guidance of them. I was terrified that my children might become victims of a paedophile, as I had done. I was all too aware of how manipulative paedophiles can be, and how easy it can be not to realise as a child the harm that they are doing. I had also always been petrified that Cooke might in some way target my kids for revenge on me. This wasn't just a part of my nightmares but a real acute fear. I tried hard to get them to understand that no one should look at or touch the private parts of their body.

Just before I went to court, I told the children I was going away for a little while.

'I want to let you know that the police have asked me to go to court to tell them about the bold man who hurt me. When people do wrong, they have to pay the price. The police want me to explain what happened so they can send him to jail.'

I wanted to explain things to them gradually, so that they didn't get a huge shock one day when they realised I had been part of a big trial. I didn't believe in burying the truth, but I knew I couldn't just blurt everything out or I'd risk scaring them or else not explaining things properly. All things considered, I don't think I am an overprotective or clingy mother, but my experience with Cooke has taught me to be very cautious.

'Is this about the kiddy fiddler?' Glenn asked me when he learned I was going back to court.

I was a bit taken aback as I had never used that term before, but he was twenty years old by then and this was his way of understanding it. He had never spoken to me about it before, but I realised he must know what had happened to me. His brothers and sister heard him say that, and from that day on Cooke was known in our house as 'the kiddy fiddler'. It wasn't ideal but I didn't want to tell them his name or anything about him so that was how it remained.

My little girl was much more inquisitive. She was only just a baby when I started the first trial and seven when I returned for the rematch with Cooke in 2007. She wanted to know exactly how the man had hurt me, and if I was okay now. I just told her that I had to help the police and that I was fine.

What greatly confused the older kids was why I had to go

back to court a second time. They already knew I had been to trial once and that Cooke had been sent to prison. Now they saw me going away again and didn't understand why. In their minds, they thought that if you told the police about a bad man and he went to prison, he stayed there. I have to say I shared some of their confusion, but try explaining to kids how a legal technicality can result in an appeal and freedom for a convicted criminal! I certainly didn't want to shake their belief in our legal system at such a young and vulnerable age. I wanted them to be able to believe the bad people in this world stay locked up, even when I knew the reality was not that simple.

The day that I returned home after Cooke was convicted for the second time, my youngest son Ryan had heard a news item on the radio. He knew it was about the 'bold' man I had been to court for. It nearly broke my heart when he said to me, 'Mammy, I am really, really happy for you because you have put a bold man in prison and now he can't hurt any more children. I think you have had an awful lot of courage and I am very proud of what you did. I know some people don't even have the courage to tell the police bad things.' I couldn't have had a better welcome home and reached out and cuddled him for all I was worth.

The night before, I had telephoned my children from my hotel room. We all said prayers together down the line; it had become a regular ritual while I was away and it gave me great comfort.

'Dear God, please let Mammy get justice so she can come home again and be happy with us,' Ryan had said. I'm not some big Holy Joe, but I certainly wore my knees out asking a few favours from God in the run up to Cooke's second conviction!

The kids also wanted to know all about the Four Courts, and if pictures of the courthouse came on the television, they would say, 'That's where Mammy has been.'

They were curious to know if being in court was like it was in television programmes. Apart from American shows, the only court dramas we ever watched on television were *Kavanagh QC* and the occasional court scene in *The Bill*. I told the kids that the judge and the barristers wore wigs like on the telly, but that was where the similarities ended! I said real-life court was much slower. I didn't share with them just how scary it could also be.

After the sentencing, we went to Malta for a family holiday and it was heaven. It was also a time for healing. The kids had a blast and I had the chance to relax without thinking about Cooke, court cases or sentences. It was as if I had been living in two different worlds for years. In one breath I was giving evidence in the formal surroundings of a courtroom, and the next I was back home in the bosom of my family, trying to forge on with a normal life. It was always worth facing the horror of that courtroom, though, just so I could return to the hustle and bustle of a happy, noisy family life where I knew my children were safe because I was fighting to put a terrible man behind bars.

Recently I told the children I was going to write a book about my life. I told them I was doing it so that people would point at the bold man in the street and not point at Mammy. 'Why would they point at you, Mammy? You have done a good thing. You haven't done anything wrong,' Ryan replied. I am delighted they have developed such a keen sense of what is right and what is wrong. My children most certainly missed me when I was away at both trials but they also knew I was fighting for a good cause. They are all bright, spirited and decent youngsters, and as a result settled back easily into our normal routine once the last trial was over.

As they are all different ages, they have dealt with the impact in differing ways, but if they want to know more I will be ready to explain what happened, at the appropriate time in their life. They have all shown me great support and encouragement throughout the two trials and I am very proud of the way they have grown up to be principled and strong despite the shadow hanging over us for so many years. The whole process started when my eldest son was a young boy, and now he has graduated from college. I missed one of Cian's birthdays because I was away from home giving evidence in Dublin. My daughter was christened when my fight against Cooke began, and it ended when she had made her first Holy Communion. It was virtually impossible for me to plan a holiday or do anything social during the years when court proceedings were in progress. I was always waiting on something – a court hearing or an appeal date – the list was endless.

It wasn't just my own children I tried to protect. As well as Mammy and Daddy, I always tried to shield my brothers and sister. Our family struggle is still going on because everyone in it was affected by Cooke's abuse of me. I always tried to maintain a positive outlook on the legal battle, but sometimes I just felt like I was wasting my time; I would be lying if I said otherwise. I had never discussed the details of my abuse with my siblings because I was the eldest child and always wanted to look after them. While Mammy and Daddy came to court, I didn't want my brothers and sister to see me there, but they insisted on turning up on occasions to show me their support, and I will be forever grateful to them for that. Nonetheless, I didn't want them to see me hurting because they had always previously seen me as the strong one.

Something changed during those years. For the first time, I saw how much they wanted to protect *me* and I realised there was nothing they wouldn't do to take away my pain. I knew they could never do that because it was something I had to deal with myself, but I will never forget the looks on their faces when they turned up in court and heard the terrible details of what had happened to their big sister.

During the first trial, I don't think anyone in my family fully understood how much Cooke had affected my life because I'd kept so much to myself in an effort to spare their emotions. But by the time the second trial came around, there were no taboo subjects left. I could no longer pretend to be the big protector when they saw me in the dock, destroyed and humiliated all over again by having to detail what Cooke had done to me. The difference was that now I could lean on them instead of feeling I should be trying to protect them.

Every one of my siblings is an individual person, with different qualities and faults. I love each of them the same, and they all show me their love in different ways. Despite the rows and the tear ups we have, my family remains close and united. Words don't always cover what you need to know. So often, it has been how my family have treated me, and not what they have said, that has counted the most.

Mammy always supported her other children, too, but she hid a lot of her own pain over what happened to me. On the last day of the trial, when Cooke was convicted, Mammy's sister came into court to support her. She had never sat down with my auntie and described what had happened to me, but that day my auntie heard for herself the details of Cooke's abuse as the judge summed up the case before the jury. Mammy was stunned when her sister broke down and sobbed. Mammy had heard the details so many times by then that they didn't have the same impact on her as they had done during the first trial. She'd begun to question if she was becoming anaesthetised to the full horror. Her comfort was that she finally had someone in her own family who knew what she had silently suffered for so many years. It gave her the opportunity to be able to speak freely and honestly about what had happened to her daughter. She no longer had to 'leave well alone'.

When Cooke was freed from his first trial on a technicality, Mammy lost all faith in the legal system. She didn't understand how or why it could happen. But when he was convicted on the second trial, she almost had more faith in the system because it had persisted in seeing that justice was upheld. The Catholic Church had wounded and hurt Mammy over the years but, like me, she had always kept her faith in God and prayed constantly for justice. When she first heard about the retrial she didn't think about herself. Her first thoughts were for her daughter and how I would react. However badly Mammy had been hurt, her own feelings always took a back seat to mine because she never lost sight of the fact that she was my mother and I was, in essence, still her little girl. On the last day in court, she told me she was filled with pride. She had one arm around her sister and the other around her daughter. She looked up and saw her husband, her sons and her other daughter, and realised that we had got through everything as a family. She left court with tears rolling down her cheeks, but they were tears of relief and happiness. She believed justice had finally been served.

The only thing that hurt her was when Cooke's defence barrister told the judge that Cooke did not accept the court's decision and that he insisted he was an innocent man. She wanted to say to him, 'When you meet your Maker, you will find out how innocent you are because God speaks before us all.'

She spoke with some of the jury members afterwards and their words gave her great comfort. They told her how courageous they thought I had been and how they had believed me from the moment I gave evidence. They also said they recognised the pain she had gone through as a mother and saw that she had always been there for me. It was these words from ordinary people that mattered the most to Mammy.

18

For all of Cooke's victims, the journey has been a long one. For us, it didn't start in the Four Courts of justice but way back when we were still too young to understand what was going on. The judicial process was incredibly tough and none of it would have been possible had it not been for the determination and hard work of the Gardaí involved in bringing the case against Cooke. It was also a tough job for them, raking over the terrible past of innocent lives which had been so badly damaged by one man's insatiable and twisted desires. This book would not be complete without the views of one man who made the journey alongside us, so I want to include here the story of a man who helped to make a tremendous difference to so many lives, probably more even than he realises.

In his own words here is Detective Inspector Gerry Kelly's story:

As far as we can establish, Eamonn Cooke began his litany of crimes in a very old-fashioned and insular community during the 1970s. To have any chance of understanding how he got away with his crimes for so long, you have to begin by getting into the very specific mindset of society at the time. The word 'paedophile' didn't enter the Irish vocabulary until the 1990s when the whole clerical sex abuse scandal erupted. In the 1970s, child abuse was not something Irish society could even comprehend. It sounds naive, even as I say it, but it was the truth. If you said bad things about priests or anyone in authority, you were likely to be locked away in an institution like the Magdalen Laundries, the infamous and often brutal homes run by the nuns.

In the course of my work, I heard about a woman who in 1964 walked into one of the main police stations in Dublin City and reported that she had been sexually abused and raped as a young girl by a priest. She was literally run out of the station and chased down the streets by Gardaí who were furious at her. They said she was a disgrace for making up such scandalous and scurrilous accusations about a member of the clergy. It took her another thirty years before she felt able to go back and report the abuse to police a second time, only this time she was believed. She revealed how humiliated and frightened she'd been by her experience with the police on that first occasion. The sad fact of life was that back then no one in Ireland was prepared to believe that this sort of crime took place.

In Siobhan's case, there was not only the time that she lived in to factor in, but also the fact that Cooke also happened to be a very cunning and manipulative man. In the end, he proved to be quite a formidable force. Few of the detectives who met him realised that when we first took him on.

He had always been a bit of an enigma, but certainly I am not aware of any police suspicions about his child abuse before he was arrested in the 90s. If anything, some detectives were shocked because he was such a well-known figure. One or two even questioned if a mistake had been made, but as we delved deeper into our investigation, it soon became very clear that we were not wrong about him. I had come across him a few times previously but not for any sinister reason. I think there may have been a bit of bother with a neighbour or something, but it wasn't a crime that had any relevance to his abuse.

He was always a natural rebel. In an article which he wrote about himself, he says he was born into a Republican family on 4 November 1936 and was one of four children. His mother once belonged to an organisation called Cumann na mBhan, the female wing of the IRA of the time, and was involved in supporting the men during the Civil War, running messages and errands. On some occasions she was said to have carried guns.

It was a natural progression that Cooke himself would end up somewhere within the ranks of the

Republican movement and in the 1950s he was part of an active service unit. As part of the criminal activities of that group, he was jailed in 1957 for five years for possession of a firearm, shooting with intent and shop breaking. This followed a shoot out with Gardaí. Cooke and a team hired a car and set off for Bray where they were going to carry out a robbery at a petrol station. Gardaí ambushed them and shots were fired at police. Cooke escaped on foot and was later arrested. He refused to plead guilty and was sent to Mountjoy Prison before being transferred to Portlaoise Jail, where paramilitaries are held.

He learned his criminal ways young and once described how he blew up a monument in Glasnevin Cemetery on the north side of Dublin. He said he was only twelve when he constructed a pipe bomb and lobbed it on to the top of the O'Connell monument in the graveyard. He then climbed over a gate and lit a candle fuse to blow up the bomb. It exploded and some damage was caused to windows in nearby properties. Cooke was caught and fined £40.

Before investigating Cooke, I had been involved in a few cases of sexual assault while still working as a uniformed officer. Sex crimes are not the type of thing you readily volunteer for but, as I had some limited experience of this type of work, the Cooke investigation fell into my lap. Initially, it had no special significance to me but eventually

Cooke was arrested and questioned about the allegations being made against him. He immediately denied the allegations but he didn't take the stance that he refused to answer our questions.

Over the years, I learned that Cooke was brilliant at weaving a lot of lies together with a little truth. There was always a huge smokescreen between what he said and what was reality. That became his pattern over a series of police interviews. He had got away with so much over time but we believed we had a strong enough case against him. We sent our files off to the DPP, which is responsible for deciding whether or not to bring a case to court.

From the very beginning, Siobhan warned me that Cooke was evil and manipulative but I don't think I realised how cunning he was until a significant way through our investigations and trials. I remember the first time she called me and we made an arrangement to meet at Bewleys Hotel. Siobhan didn't want to make a statement in the early days but her information prompted a much bigger investigation because it brought a lot more people into the picture. One woman agreed to make a statement immediately and was clearly very ready to do so. Then in January of 2000, Louise Tyrrell and I went back to Siobhan and asked her if she would consider going forward. We left the decision with her. An enquiry team had been set up by now and was based at Ronanstown

Garda Station. Officers had to cross-reference all the information that was starting to come in. I don't think Cooke knew that the case against him was building to such a large degree. We chipped away quietly to get as much information as possible.

I remember meeting Siobhan's parents with her and having to explain that the rules of evidence meant that I couldn't simply take her information and go to court with it. I explained that she would have to go to court and place that evidence before a judge and jury. She had hoped that I would be able to take her information and build a case against Cooke without her having to go further. I understood that she was frightened. It was a natural way for her to feel because Cooke had caused her so much hurt, not just as a child but in her adult life as well. It was hard to put across to Siobhan that she would be expected to give the most intimate details of her abuse to a courtroom. I could see that she was panicked and uncomfortable, but it was my professional duty to make sure she understood everything, exactly what it would take to get a conviction on Cooke.

Siobhan's parents were naturally very nervous, too. Their first instinct was to protect their daughter, especially after everything she had been through. They were worried about the impact a trial might have on her as they had already seen her suffer emotionally. Our job at that meeting was to be as honest as we could about what court entailed and what we would need her to do as a witness. We had to be upfront and honest with them all because it would have been wrong to take a statement from Siobhan and only then tell her what she was going to face in court. She had a million questions about court procedure. In particular, she wanted to know who would be asking her questions. Siobhan had a huge advantage as a potential witness because she has the memory of a computer. She could recall the events in Cooke's house as clearly as if they had taken place the day before. We believed that would stand her in good stead when she came to be cross-examined.

By this stage, we already had two witnesses. One was a young boy and the second was the woman who had previously come forward. We were also speaking with two sisters who had come forward with allegations of the same nature against Cooke. Our case was getting stronger and we did try to emphasise to Siobhan that she was not alone anymore. She had explained to Louise and me that she had always felt she was trying to battle Cooke on her own. We told her that the other witnesses were making the same allegations against him, and that together they would all be great.

The police team was extremely determined in the way they set about their investigation. We were all very positive and wanted to make sure we got the right conviction. We were all certain by this stage that we were dealing with a very dangerous man. We were confident that we could get a conviction because our witnesses were good; they were mature and articulate and came from good backgrounds. There was nothing that could weaken them in terms of their character. What was most crucial was that their stories were remarkably similar even though some abuses had been committed in the 70s and others in the 80s. The pattern of abuse remained the same and so there was a thread linking all these victims, even though some of them had never met.

Fear had always been the thing that had prevented these girls from coming forward, and when we met them we could see that Cooke still had that hold over them. This became a big issue in the first trial when the girls were forced to prove they still feared Cooke. Sadly, it meant that two further witnesses who'd come forward were ruled out of the trial because the court found they had not proved their fear. This was quite a blow because I had always believed that these two girls were, if anything, the people whose lives had been most affected by Cooke. The majority of one girl's family do not know to this day that she was one of his victims, and during the trial she took a day off work every day until the end so she could go and sit with the other witnesses to support them.

The other woman had suffered immeasurably.

I thought it was very hard for that one particular woman. It was as if she had put up a barrier many years ago to protect herself from the damage Cooke had inflicted on her. Now it seemed impossible for her to bring it down again. For that reason, I suspect she was unable to explain to a psychologist what exactly she had suffered. Consequently, her report said she was unable to prove fear of her abuser. She was trying to keep the abuse buried even though I felt she had been terribly affected.

These are hard cases to deal with for detectives. It doesn't compare to what the victims go through but, nonetheless, officers can be affected, especially when it comes to crimes against children. They are human beings at the end of the day, not robots, and they wouldn't be normal if they didn't react. If you didn't feel for these women then you couldn't have a heart or soul. Cooke didn't make it any easier for his victims because he fought the charges tooth and nail, all the way. He showed no compassion or admission of guilt, which would have spared them going through not just one trial, but two, and numerous High Court appeal bids.

What struck us all was how Cooke had been able to get away with his crimes for so long. The police knew nothing about his child abuse for decades. Then it was as if someone had come along and unlocked a cupboard crammed with his crimes. They all seemed to pour out at once from different directions. This may have been because public awareness regarding abuse was now very high. There were cases in the media almost daily and these no doubt prompted victims to come forward.

We interviewed many more people than just the witnesses who got through. Some still denied they were abused but it was obvious they were too frightened to speak out. I remember re-interviewing one victim who threatened me with legal action because she was so afraid of Cooke.

As the investigation continued, it took on a snowball effect; the more people we interviewed, the more names we collected of people who had been abused by Cooke. Another clear message that came through was the threats he made in the latter years of their abuse. Several of the victims remembered clearly how Cooke had said he would show their parents photographs of them in their underwear if they opened their mouths about the abuse or stopped coming to his house. He was trying to blame them and make them feel guilty for what *he* was doing.

In the end we went to trial with four of the six female witnesses who'd come forward. The boy withdrew his statement before a solicitor, saying he had made the story up. When we got the first conviction, it was brilliant. It had been a tense trial and we certainly had our moments. At times, things went against us and we were worried it wasn't going to happen. When he got ten years we were delighted. A lot of people say he should have got a lot more, and I agree, but in terms of the powers that courts have to sentence paedophiles, it was a great sentence. Cooke never showed a dot of emotion but he must have been shocked. We were all convinced that he thought he was going to beat the case. He had shown arrogance and confidence throughout the hearing. I don't know if this was because he had got away with his crimes for so long, but his sentence certainly brought him down to earth. Cooke didn't have to take the stand during the trial. He was not required to give evidence or be cross-examined, but couldn't keep quiet and just sit in the dock.

As hard as the case was, we knew it was our job. A ten-year sentence on Cooke was a great result because we all felt that one of the most important things was to protect the lives of vulnerable children. Sending Cooke to jail certainly helped to do that. Up until that point, he had beaten the system at every turn and had managed to wriggle out of a great many accusations over the years. His crimes had finally caught up with him, though. There was a sense of great pride among his victims because they had stood up to him, taken him on and beaten him, despite his constant protestations of innocence. I remember saying to the women that the truth always wins. This was a victory for honesty and for truth, and the detectives shared their joy.

There was a great party that night and a good few drinks were sunk to celebrate the result of the case. There were the police officers, the women themselves, their extended families and even some of the members of the jury. Money couldn't have bought the feel-good factor experienced that evening – it was better than winning the Lottery. You don't get that feeling in my job very often, but when it comes along you savour it. It was certainly one of the highlights of my career.

But there was a huge sense of frustration when Cooke walked free on a technicality. A lot of time and effort had gone into securing his conviction and yet he had managed to beat the system once again. There was very little anyone could do because the required warning that should have been given to the jury had been forgotten. The whole team was deeply disappointed to know Cooke was out on the streets again. We tried to object to his bail again on the grounds of his previous attempts at intimidation of Siobhan, but our application for a remand in custody was refused on the grounds that it had been some years since he had made any approaches to her. Siobhan had been very frightened when he turned up at her work, on both occasions. She had to go to the High Court and give evidence against him, so she has faced him plenty of times across a courtroom.

After our first victory turned out to be only temporary there was huge despondency because most people felt there was little hope for a retrial. We only had Siobhan left as a witness at that stage, and without another it was felt unlikely that a second trial would be successful. Thankfully, the DPP thought it was in the public interest to go for a retrial but it was still a worrying time, because we had significantly fewer witnesses the second time around. A second witness had come forward so that at least strengthened the case. What we hadn't bargained on was how strong those two witnesses would turn out to be.

By this stage, they were well used to the court system. They had given evidence on a number of occasions and they had belief in themselves. Their job wasn't any easier, but they had more confidence when they had to take the stand. Both women were absolutely brilliant when they gave their evidence. They were cool, calm and articulate, and they were particularly good during their cross-examination. At one stage, Cooke's defence counsel said to one of the women, 'I put it to you that Eamonn Cooke did not, in any way, molest you or touch you.' She replied, 'Well, if he didn't, would you have any suggestions who did?' It was that kind of quick thinking and response that was so different from the first trial. It had a powerful effect on the whole room, including the jury.

The women gave their evidence very differently, but each was as effective as the other. It was quite an emotional time in the courtroom. Siobhan got understandably very flustered and embarrassed at one point, when she had to describe Cooke's abuse, and my heart went out to her. The judge offered her a break so that she could compose herself.

The second trial dragged on for so long. There were legal points to debate in the absence of the jury and then there was the delay when Cooke came into court with his injury. We thought we would never get to the end of it. When we finally got the result, in some ways it was even more satisfying than the first trial because we had so much stacked against us. It was a feeling beyond compare.

I think Cooke is an intelligent but devious man. I also think he is a very, very cunning man, but if I had to sum him up in one word, I would say he is evil. He is a very formidable force. He groomed each and every one of the children he abused before he carried out sexual acts. Crucially, he won their trust and that trust was ultimately betrayed. He gave them sweets and money. Some of his victims said he had a grandfatherly approach and he bought one a teddy bear. Then, when he had them in his clutches, he installed fear into them to keep them as his victims. He told Siobhan that he could see her everywhere she went and when she saw him putting up an aerial on the telegraph pole outside her house she believed him.

I have the utmost admiration for all the women who came forward and stood up to Cooke. They showed great courage and tenacity throughout. When they asked me for help, I just told them to tell the truth. That was all anyone could ask them to do. For me it was a triumph for good over evil, for right over wrong. It was what I signed up to do.

19

The cost of the criminal trials that finally put Eamonn Cooke behind bars ran into millions and millions of pounds. I am not even sure the State could accurately pinpoint just how much was spent to ensure that he remained a convicted and imprisoned paedophile. What I do know is that not a single penny of it was wasted in making the world a safer place from a sexual deviant of the worst kind.

It has been a turbulent and difficult path for all Cooke's victims and our respective families. Sometimes we thought the nightmare was never going to end. For my part, I have never regretted going forward because I never doubted that Cooke would reoffend and continue to ravage the innocence of children so long as he had breath left in his body and was allowed to roam free. I didn't pursue him just to avenge the abuse he inflicted on me. Those days are long gone and I can never change what happened to me. I was given the chance to stop him from hurting more young children in the future, and that was my most important reason for seeking justice.

In my eyes, his convictions for crimes against me also represent justice for each and every child who was ever harmed at his hands. They may not have had their day in court but they know who they are. For every day Cooke remains behind bars they need no longer be afraid.

I have had extraordinary support along the way. Mammy and Daddy were at my side throughout, as was my husband Derek and my family who gave me such unswerving loyalty at all times. I would never have made it through without their help. I also had amazing love and support from Breda Allen of the Rape Crisis Centre in Dublin as well as from Deirdre Fitzpatrick from One In Four. They not only gave me legal advice but provided me with an emotional safety net at times when I needed it the most.

I played my part in convicting Cooke, but it would not be right to tell this story without paying tribute to Pat McCarthy and Isobel Kennedy. Without their wisdom and superb knowledge of the law, I am sure Cooke would still be a free man. Pat McCarthy has now become a High Court judge and I am confident that the legal hierarchy and the Irish public have gained a great asset at the most senior level.

In 2000, when I made my fateful decision to give a statement against Cooke, I had no faith left in any State, legal or public institution. I had been let down by so many professional bodies that I believed no one cared that Cooke was still out there violating children. When Gerry Kelly asked me to consider making a statement against Cooke, I had no reason to consider that he was any different from all the rest. I was wrong. All the police in this case cared deeply about securing a conviction against Cooke. Detective Inspector Todd O'Loughlin started the investigation and led a highly professional team of police officers. He has since retired but I would like to publicly thank him for all he did. Gerry Kelly and Louise Tyrrell were the first officers I came into contact with and they were brilliant. I couldn't have asked for more from them. They were not the only ones; Detective Garda Dennis Kenny, Detective Garda Robert Cooper and Detective Garda Kevin Walsh and Garda Fiona O'Dowd all formed part of that team and deserve recognition for the determination and professionalism they put into securing Cooke's conviction. Detective Garda Dennis Kenny has since tragically died, suddenly and unexpectedly, in February 2008. I would like to pay special tribute to him for his support and friendship to all my family. He will be sorely missed and may he rest in peace.

I know that the details of what Cooke did to all his victims in this case had a profound effect on the detectives involved. They had a professional job to do and, at times, it must have been very hard to deal with Cooke, knowing the crimes he had committed. They all treated me with the utmost humanity and care over the years that I worked with them. I will always be grateful for their kindness and patience at some of the most testing periods of my life. I know that on occasions they bore the backlash of my frustrations and fury as we met pitfalls along the way, but I know they shared those difficult times with me. More importantly, I salute their tenacity in pursuing justice. The odds were often stacked against us, but they never gave up trying to put the bad man away. Despite the hurdles, their hard work paid off and I will never be able to thank them enough. All of them are a credit to their profession.

I reserve special thanks for Gerry Kelly for his unstinting

support throughout. He was my rock throughout all the times I had to go to court, including Cooke's numerous attempts to overturn his conviction in the High Court. Gerry was the one who patiently tried to explain the things I didn't understand about the legal process. He was always there for me to lean on throughout our difficult seven-year battle. He witnessed every emotion in me: fear, anger, jubilation and exhaustion. He saw the snot and tears and never batted an eyelid. I will never be able to thank him enough for his friendship and his outstanding professionalism. I know I emerged a different person from the trials and I am sure they had their effect on Gerry too.

The police are not psychologists and yet they are the ones who are left to pick up the pieces of victims like me. They are left to answer our questions about what is going on in court around us because we have no one else to turn to. That is the fault of our legal system, which fails to look after witnesses, and of the politicians who fail to amend it. The police have to put up with an awful lot of grief from victims of crime because they have no one else on whom to vent their frustration. They also wrongly get the blame for the faults of a judicial system that sometimes lets victims down. They are the first line of defence when someone is the victim of a crime, but the decent men and women in the police force don't sign up to shoulder the blame for the inadequacies of a State that has not yet provided a satisfactory level of care for victims. Until our politicians wise up to the failings in our legal system, many victims and witnesses will remain unwilling to become a part of the judicial process. I have always believed there should be a Victim's Charter, to look after the welfare of those who have been wronged. Currently, our legal system is heavily weighted in favour of the accused. The new charter should include a victim's automatic right to a State-funded legal representative throughout all criminal proceedings.

The Irish Government also needs to provide more funding for the statutory organisations that deal with victims of sex crimes. In particular, hard cash needs to be allocated to the police service to provide appropriate victim-centred facilities where victims of crime can be interviewed, especially in cases of sex crimes. Funds are also needed to provide an after-care service for those who have reported sexual crimes to the police. In many cases, such victims have nowhere to turn in their hour of need.

The Dublin-based charity One in Four, already mentioned in this book, has been a tower of strength for me in my recovery. It is so-called because it is estimated that one in four children in Ireland has been, or will be, violently or sexually abused. These are terrifying statistics that shame all of Ireland. It is a charity that is severely underfunded, as is the Rape Crisis Centre.

I think ordinary people would be horrified if they realised how many men and women have been abused as children. I cannot stress enough the importance of groups like these in helping people to survive. These two charities helped to turn my life around. They gave me the support to face up to the terrible things that happened in my childhood. They taught me that I was not to blame for what happened to me and that all the guilt I buried inside did not belong to me. Their amazing counsellors also gave me hope.

I know I am one of the lucky ones in that I have survived. I have emotional battle scars but I am still in one piece. Others were not so lucky; many victims of abuse take their own lives or become enslaved to drink or drugs just to make it through the day. Mental illness, such as self-harming, schizophrenia and multiple personality disorder, often manifests as a result of untreated sexual abuse. That is why groups like this need more government funding, because they are where the damaged and tortured souls seek help.

There is an ocean of suffering in my country, some of which will never be charted. In the 70s and 80s, it was as if society had a secret door behind which it hid all the gruesome details of the widespread abuse that was going on. No one wanted to open up that door for fear of what might come out. It wasn't until the 90s that the full horrors of systematic abuse and failure to investigate by those in authority really came to light. Now we are raking over the decaying, rotting bones of our shameful history.

There are parts of my story that, for legal reasons, I still cannot disclose, but in the fullness of time those details may also become public knowledge. I hope so. I am still angry that professional organisations such as the clergy covered up for Cooke when they knew he was a danger to children. I will never understand how a Christian organisation can live with its conscience after such behaviour.

One thing that gave me great comfort in the second trial was the way the judge delivered her summing up. She made it very clear she understood the mind-set of the 1970s. She accepted that it was a very different era, one when adults still believed their children could roam freely without coming to any harm.

Mammy also took great comfort from the judge's words. We often hear about the ordeals of children abused by paedophiles, but who hears the stories of the mammies and the other family members who have to live with the consequences of something so terrible happening to their relative? I was not the only victim of Cooke in my family. All of us suffered as a result of what he did to me, and many of the other children who were hurt echo my feelings on this. I felt the judge understood this, and am grateful that she made me feel that I was not just part of the court process. Instead, to her I was a human being caught up in a tragedy that deeply affected my family too. She saw the support I received from loved ones who turned up to court to be with me every day, and paid recognition to those people at the end of the trial. No one can ever really measure the human cost to families of the deeds perpetrated by the likes of Cooke, but I have always compared it to throwing a stone into a still pond. The ripples spread far and wide, well beyond the obvious target.

As a man and as a father, Daddy has always found Cooke's abuse of his daughter particularly difficult to deal with and still struggles with it today. But I know he has always loved me and been there for me through some of my darkest days. It has been difficult for him to accept how any man could abuse a child, especially his daughter, but the love between us has never been in question and I know he has always been very proud of me. Those are the most important things.

I will never understand the mind of a paedophile but I do

know that, in Cooke's world, it is normal and appropriate to have sexual relations with young children. He bought one of his victims a Valentine's card and flowers and told her that he loved her when she was still just a child. He even told her he had chosen the names of their future children. That is why he will always remain a danger until the day he dies, and why he has no place in a civilised and decent society. He doesn't see the harm he inflicts deep within the lives of his victims; has no remorse for his crimes. He does, however, know that society views his actions as wrong and has always taken whatever measures he can to avoid detection. He thought he was invincible, but was proved wrong. I don't believe Cooke will ever feel a shred of conscience for his crimes, and if ever he tried to write down the names of all the children he has harmed, I am sure he would die of old age before he could reach the end. I will never know exactly how many children he abused, but he committed his crimes for at least thirty years, possibly many more. My strongest hope and belief is that he is withering away now in prison because he is prevented from molesting children. It was all he ever lived for and I have not an ounce of compassion for the faltering body or mind of a man who caused so much pain to innocent young people.

It wasn't until the trials that I discovered from one of his other victims that Cooke once set up a 'childline' for abused and vulnerable children. I cannot imagine anything more sinister or disturbing. It made my blood boil and I shudder to think that vulnerable children may unwittingly have called upon such a monster for help at a time when they needed rescuing the most. It was always his ploy to appear in public as a huge supporter of children's causes. He pretended to be their best friend when in reality he was their worst nightmare.

Another victim revealed how he would deliver Easter eggs to children's orphanages. I later found a very old newspaper clipping of Cooke and the crew from Radio Dublin. A photograph shows the youngsters all sitting on top of one of his Jaguars, emblazoned with the Radio Dublin logo along the side. The DJs look like any high-spirited motley crew of young people having the time of their lives. Cooke, wearing his trademark dark suit, is standing alongside his team. The article was published on 6 April 1978, just days before James led the walk-out of the station. It reported all the news from Radio Dublin and included references to Cooke's Easter Egg donations. It read: 'Radio Dublin is proud to relate their successful Easter Egg campaign for orphanages. The appeal was launched last Wednesday and already, after a few days, they have collected enough eggs to go round several orphanages as well as Our Lady's Hospital for Sick Children.'

Cooke is even alleged to have staged a contest for dozens of junior majorettes. He sat on the judges' panel and watched the youngsters go through their paces. It is horrifying to think that such an evil man was able to orchestrate access to children right up until he was finally caught in his sixties.

I know that after sacrificing my anonymity with this book, people will ask me questions about the Cooke case and raise further important issues about child sex abuse. I am more than comfortable to tackle all this because I know I will never again face anything as terrible as Cooke's abuse of me or the terrifying ordeal of giving evidence against him in court.

I waited a long time for the chance to speak out about this. It sounds like a cliché, but if this book helps just one person who has suffered in the same way as Cooke's victims, then it will have been worth the wait. I have tried to explain how I got over my own experience, with the love of family and friends and the help of superb support groups. I hope the trials and the publicity surrounding them have given hope to other victims of abuse. At the end of Cooke's sentencing in 2007, a woman I have never met came up to me and said I had changed her life by coming forward to testify against him. She confided she had been sexually abused when she was a child and, as a result of reading about Cooke's trial, had finally gone to get counselling for the suffering she had endured.

Some abuse victims never get over their ordeal; they feel it is torture to be alive still, and I have been in that place too, not wanting to tell a soul how you feel or what has happened to you. I sought help and was turned away, which had a terrible impact on me. Since the two trials I have been approached by a lot of people who have told me they were similarly abused. They have asked for my help and I always tell them the best they can get is from the Rape Crisis Centre or One in Four because I am not a qualified professional counsellor. But while I cannot give professional advice, I will always listen to other people's stories because I know how much it means just to be able to talk to someone who is willing to believe you. I know I cannot solve everyone's problems, as much as I would like to, but I hope I can make a difference, no matter how small.

It took seven years to get a final conviction against Cooke.

During those years he launched numerous legal actions in the Court of Criminal Appeal, which finally resulted in his retrial. All that time, I could not open my mouth and say a word about the man for legal reasons. It is important for me to have a public voice now because I want to speak out, not only for existing victims, but to lobby for changes in the law to protect future victims. Today, I not only have my freedom from Cooke, but the right to choose to let the public know my story. It is important for everyone to know how evil and manipulative people like him are; it is important for people to know what child sex abuse victims go through. In particular, I want to draw attention to the apparently benign and silent crime of grooming that still goes widely unrecognised in Ireland. In Britain, there are already laws against grooming which make it a criminal offence.

Grooming is as complicit, dangerous and sinister as the act of abuse itself. It is a crime that enables paedophiles to prepare children to undergo gross sexual acts for an abuser's gratification. Groomers attract then attack children when they are at their most vulnerable.

There is still not sufficient understanding of the nature of grooming to provide even the flimsiest of defence for children most at risk from these sexual deviants. Cooke groomed his victims as far back as the 1970s, and the nature of grooming has changed since then because of the new times we live in. If we are to stand any chance of preventing paedophiles from carrying out attacks on children, then the law must wake up to this insidious crime. I am heartened to learn of the education about such things that my children are now receiving in school. As I mentioned earlier, one of the mantras they have been taught is, 'Never let a touch be a secret.' It gives me great hope that we are finally learning from the mistakes of our past.

I can now shake off the stigma of a shame that was never mine. It belongs firmly with Eamonn Cooke and, to a much lesser degree, the society I lived in – one that found it easier to keep silent, turn a blind eye, and harshly judge those who were least to blame. I am very proud that I acted to change things, and while I knew it would be hard, was prepared to take the consequences of my actions. No one forced me to go forward against Cooke but I have not a single regret about the last seven years. No matter what people have to say about my story, I know I have done nothing wrong.

Mammy, who was once so terrified of what neighbours and community leaders might think of her family, is now one of my staunchest supporters and if anyone asks her about the whole Cooke saga, she stands up and fights my corner. She is proud to tell people that I spent seven years battling the man.

I want people to know what it feels like to go and face your abuser in court. I want to highlight the fact that our political system has a duty to do more to protect innocent witnesses who come forward to secure convictions against the evil people living among us. My primary reason for going to court at the turn of the Millennium was because I saw Cooke with innocent young children. I truly believed he was still abusing because he'd abused children decade after decade after decade. Now, finally, I feel I am almost free. I know I will never be totally free until the day he dies, and I trust he does so before I do because, God forgive me, I want to be the first person in Ireland to dance on his grave. I suspect there may be a long queue behind me.

The strength and courage of all his victims who came forward is no less than mine. During both trials, and since Cooke was convicted, I have received huge support from many of them. I want to send a special message of love to one girl that I cannot name. She knows who she is. When Cooke was convicted for the second time, there were far more than just two of his victims watching his downfall in that courtroom.

I know what it is like to be a victim of a paedophile but I no longer live my life as a victim. I want others to know that if they can summon the courage to reach out, just a little bit, and ask for help, there is a light at the end of that very dark tunnel. I was shocked when I discovered that I was suffering from Post Traumatic Stress Disorder so many years after I was abused. I think I had experienced the symptoms for so long that I believed they were normal. Flashbacks, mood swings and depression were so routine for me that I thought everyone felt that way. Counselling and treatment taught me that my mind would always trip me up if I allowed it to. I had to change my way of thinking, and I don't believe that can happen unless you talk to someone qualified to help you. Today I feel happier than I have ever felt before. I can go to sleep at night without nightmares because I feel a new sense of empowerment; I know there can be a good life after abuse. Today I realise what it is to be truly alive and happy. Today I am looking forward to a bright new future and hope I can use my experience to continue to help other victims of abuse. I am also looking forward to a peaceful new chapter in my life, knowing I will never again have to live in the dark shadow of someone else's shame.

I have a very happy marriage and four wonderful children whom I love very much. I love the work I do and am planning to expand my music business, now that I have the confidence to go forward in my life. I want to travel then sit back and enjoy the rest of my life. Cooke is not on my mind every day, or every week, but every now and again something comes up and my heart misses a beat. It is a lifelong burden, but unfortunately sentences on paedophiles don't take into account the way these sick people damage lives.

I know few people who have managed to get over abuse without psychiatric help. Before I sought it, the legacy of Cooke's abuse had burned a hole deep into my soul. I was constantly trying to fill that hole until I realised it was not my fault. I know how such emotional pain can be buried deep in the heart of anyone who has suffered in this way. I have immense compassion for all who have been through such abuse and torment. When I see a stranger sitting at the side of a busy street with a begging bowl, I just know they have not arrived there by accident. Somehow, life has dealt them a bad hand and that human being crying out for kindness is someone's son or someone's daughter. Those who step over the vulnerable people on our streets never bother to find out what has happened in their lives to put them there.

Cooke will get out of prison at some point unless he dies in jail, and I don't know if God is going to be that good to me. But if he is released, he will be back on the streets of Ireland living among decent families. If he is ever released from prison, he has to go and live somewhere and it is my belief that the community he slides into should know everything about the man who is coming to live among them. My story has been written to let those people know the truth about a man who might one day be their neighbour. For too many years, Eamonn Cooke was my biggest nightmare, in more ways than one. The tables have turned now. I intend to be his.

Acknowledgements

Thank you to my mammy, Kathleen, for her constant love, care and guidance throughout my life and for being by my side every day in court. Thanks also to my daddy, Liam, for his unstinting love and pride in his daughter. To my brothers, Robert, Kieran, and David, and my sister, Adrienne, for their reassurance and unconditional love and for helping to put the smile back on my face when I am down.

I will always be grateful to the victims of Eamonn Cooke who have supported me in telling my story. You have shared this turbulent journey with me and I salute your courage and strength from which I have drawn huge inspiration.

To the countless victims of Eamonn Cooke I will never know and for survivors of abuse everywhere. I pray your darkness turns to light and your conflict turns to peace.

I will never be able to repay Breda Allen, formerly at the Rape Crisis Centre, and Deirdre Fitzpatrick at One in Four. You will never know how much you helped me in my darkest hours.

To my biographer Rosie Dunn and her partner Billy Griffiths for believing in me. Without their help and support this book would never have been possible. Thanks for the laughs, too!

To my literary agent Robert Smith and all at Random House, especially commissioning editor Emma Rose who has been a joy to work with.

I will never forget Detective Inspector Gerry Kelly and his team of detectives or Pat McCarthy and Isobel Kennedy who successfully prosecuted Eamonn Cooke twice. Thank you all for your commitment and dedication in seeking justice.

Finally, to all the many family, friends and neighbours of whom there are too many to mention by name, for standing by me through the years. I will never forget the love, kindness and, above all, patience shown to me.